IANNIS XENAKIS: *KRAANERG*

Iannis Xenakis: *Kraanerg*

JAMES HARLEY
University of Guelph, Canada

ASHGATE

© James Harley 2015

All rights reserved. No part of this publication may be reproduced, stored in a retrieval system or transmitted in any form or by any means, electronic, mechanical, photocopying, recording or otherwise without the prior permission of the publisher.

James Harley has asserted his right under the Copyright, Designs and Patents Act, 1988, to be identified as the author of this work.

Published by
Ashgate Publishing Limited
Wey Court East
Union Road
Farnham
Surrey, GU9 7PT
England

Ashgate Publishing Company
110 Cherry Street
Suite 3-1
Burlington, VT 05401-3818
USA

www.ashgate.com

British Library Cataloguing in Publication Data
A catalogue record for this book is available from the British Library.

The Library of Congress has cataloged the printed edition as follows:
Harley, James, 1959-
   Iannis Xenakis : Kraanerg / by James Harley.
       pages cm. -- (Landmarks in music since 1950)
   Includes bibliographical references and index.
   ISBN 978-1-4094-2331-7 (hardcover) 1. Xenakis, Iannis, 1922-2001. Kraanerg. I. Title.
   ML410.X45H35 2015
   780.92--dc23

2015000824

ISBN 9781409423317 (hbk)

 Printed in the United Kingdom by Henry Ling Limited,
at the Dorset Press, Dorchester, DT1 1HD

Contents

List of Figures *vii*
List of Tables *ix*
List of Music Examples *xi*
General Editor's Preface *xiii*
Acknowledgments *xv*

Introduction 1

1   Biography 3

2   Musical Background to *Kraanerg* 19

3   The *Kraanerg* Project 35

4   *Kraanerg* Analysis 53

5   Reception 103

6   Performance History 111

7   Epilogue 123

Bibliography *127*
CD Track List *131*
Index *133*

List of Figures

1.1	Iannis Xenakis, c. 1968 (Gilbert Rancy, photographer, Xenakis Archives, Bibliothèque nationale de France).	14
2.1	Group theory constraints based on rotations of a tetrahedron within a cube	27
2.2	*Polytope de Montréal* installation, French Pavilion, 1967	32
2.3	*Le Diatope*, designed by Iannis Xenakis, 1978	33
3.1	National Arts Centre, Ottawa (photographer unknown, NAC Archives)	36
3.2	Roland Petit, choreographer (photograph, National Ballet of Canada)	39
3.3	One view of stage design by Vasarely for *Kraanerg*	47
3.4	Second view of stage design by Vasarely for *Kraanerg*	47
3.5	Outline of *Kraanerg* showing basic score segments with ballet timings	50
3.6	Soloist Lynn Seymour with Pierre Elliott Trudeau, Prime Minister of Canada	51
4.1	*Kraanerg*: outline of ensemble/playback segments	64
4.2	*Kraanerg*: outline of sonic entities	68
4.3	*Kraanerg*: sketch of recorded material formal plan (Xenakis Archives)	75
4.4	Four-channel amplitude display, Playback Segment I (0:34–2:52)	76
4.5	Four-channel amplitude display, Playback Segment II (3:26–5:48)	76
4.6	Four-channel amplitude display, Playback Segment III (7:22–8:02)	77
4.7	Four-channel amplitude display, Playback Segment IV (10:18–11:18)	77
4.8	Four-channel amplitude display, Playback Segment V (13:56–15:28)	78
4.9	Four-channel amplitude display, Playback Segment VI (16:04–17:50)	78
4.10	Four-channel amplitude display, Playback Segment VII (18:10–19:32)	79
4.11	Four-channel amplitude display, Playback Segment VIII (21:48–23:00)	79
4.12	Four-channel amplitude display, Playback Segment IX (28:12–28:48)	80
4.13	Four-channel amplitude display, Playback Segment X (29:08–29:50)	80

4.14	Four-channel amplitude display, Playback Segment XI (35:20–35:52)	81
4.15	Four-channel amplitude display, Playback Segment XII (38:22–39:10)	81
4.16	Four-channel amplitude display, Playback Segment XIII (42:00–42:18)	82
4.17	Four-channel amplitude display, Playback Segment XIV (43:00–44:22)	82
4.18	Four-channel amplitude display, Playback Segment XV (47:00–47:36)	83
4.19	Four-channel amplitude display, Playback Segment XVI (48:10–48:54)	83
4.20	Four-channel amplitude display, Playback Segment XVII (52:00–58:24)	84
4.21	Four-channel amplitude display, Playback Segment XVIII (58:38–59:10)	84
4.22	Four-channel amplitude display, Playback Segment XIX (59:20–67:42)	85
4.23	Four-channel amplitude display, Playback Segment XX (69:06–75:11)	85
6.1	Image from Graeme Murphy's choreography of *Kraanerg*, featuring dancers Jan Pinkerton and Stefan Karlsson (photographer, Branco Gaica)	116
7.1	Sketches of robotic choreography by Xenakis (Xenakis Archives)	125

List of Tables

2.1	Sieve-based derivation of major scale	25
3.1	Comparison of Xenakis's *Kraanerg* instrumentation with the standard National Ballet of Canada orchestra	43
3.2	Choreographic movements for *Kraanerg* by Roland Petit	49
4.1	Timing of segments in *Kraanerg*	87
6.1	List of performances of *Kraanerg* by the National Ballet of Canada	112
6.2	List of concert performances of *Kraanerg*	114
6.3	Commercial recordings of *Kraanerg*	117

List of Music Examples

2.1	Annotated score excerpt from *Nomos alpha*	28
4.1	Page 1 of *Kraanerg* score, showing timing for the electronic part	56
4.2	Page 4 of *Kraanerg* score	57
4.3	Score excerpt of *Kraanerg*, winds material: 12:04–12:29 (p. 16)	58
4.4	Score excerpt of *Kraanerg*, continuation of winds material: 13:24–13:52 (p. 18)	59
4.5	*Kraanerg*, opening winds segment	61
4.6	*Nomos gamma*: score excerpt, mm. 409–13	73
4.7	*Kraanerg*: score excerpt showing borrowing from *Nomos gamma*, 3:02–3:18	74

General Editor's Preface to
Iannis Xenakis: Kraanerg by James Harley

Writing about compositions that draw on a number of artistic media—be they operas, vocal settings, films, or simply works blessed with descriptive titles—poses significant (and varying) challenges, as many earlier books in this series of *Landmarks in Music* have demonstrated. Dealing with aspects of a work that are not easily accessible to the reader (such as stage design, lighting, choreography and moving images, even facial expressions or bodily posture) necessarily involves the use of compromises in terms of selective photographs or the invoking of remembered experiences. Rarely is it possible (or practicable) to provide an audio-visual recording of the chosen work to accompany the musical analyses—although the CD supplied with this book goes some way to assist the reader/listener in relating the commentary to musical performance.

Such problems (and more) faced the author of this volume when he was commissioned to write about Xenakis's multimedia composition *Kraanerg*—a work itself produced to commemorate the opening of Canada's National Arts Centre in Ottawa, and first performed there on 2 June 1969, using choreography by Roland Petit and with the participation of a team of distinguished designers and dancers, in addition to the technical staff who coordinated lighting and the electronically composed sections of the score under the overall direction of the conductor, Lukas Foss. Amazingly, Petit composed his choreography without access to the music (until a few weeks before the premiere) and without there being a detailed theme or storyline, other than the rather cryptic comments made by the composer in a press-release put out by the National Arts Centre before the first performance.

I will leave it to James Harley to flesh out these generalizations, of course, for he is uniquely well qualified to introduce the reader to Iannis Xenakis's rich store of life-experiences and his development as a composer/architect of international fame. Harley is a composer himself, with specialist insights into digital music and electronic composition. He has published a biography of Xenakis and is an authority on the analysis of contemporary music. This book addresses the issues raised by a dance performance that is not exactly synchronized with the musical score, and explains the significance of its title within the context of the composer's overall output. The author presents us with an ordered series of chapters that are well researched and succinctly expressed. I warmly recommend it to you.

Wyndham Thomas
August 2014

Acknowledgments

This project was only possible with the assistance of a great many people. In the first place, Iannis Xenakis provided some sketch materials from his personal archives in Paris, assisted by Radu Stan of Éditions Salabert. Later, on a visit to North America, Xenakis answered questions, with input from his wife, Françoise. This conversation was followed up by a visit to the National Arts Centre Archives, Ottawa, where Gerry Grace provided access to press materials around the premiere of *Kraanerg* there, along with press on the opening of the NAC. This research, carried out in collaboration with Maria Anna Harley (Maja Trochimczyk), led to an article published in *Musicworks* in 1997 (Gayle Young, editor). The score of *Kraanerg*, normally only available for rental by the publisher, Boosey & Hawkes, was graciously loaned for an extended period by David Allenby, who also provided press clippings and performance history information. Correspondence, production notes, and photographs were consulted at the National Ballet of Canada Archives, Toronto (Caitlin Dyer, Adrienne Nevile, Sharon Vanderlinde). With permission from Mme Xenakis, I was able to consult the Xenakis Archives at the Bibliothèque national de France (BnF), Paris, during a research leave in 2010 from the University of Guelph. Permission to use images from this archive has been graciously facilitated by Mâkhi Xenakis. Makis Solomos, notable Xenakis scholar, facilitated access to the audio archives of the BnF. Brian Brandt (Mode Records) and Giorgio Magnanensi (Vancouver New Music) provided audio materials that were extremely valuable. I am especially grateful to Giorgio for inviting me to attend the VNM concert performance of *Kraanerg* in 2009 and participate in a post-concert discussion. Brian has graciously allowed us to include the stereo version of his excellent recording of *Kraanerg* with this book. Other Xenakis scholars who have helped me in this project in various ways include Benoît Gibson, Sharon Kanach, Gérard Pape, and Charles Turner. The University of Guelph awarded me a Summer Undergraduate Research Assistant in 2012, and Patrick Horrigan was especially helpful in producing formal charts and score transcriptions. Finally, I must express my appreciation to Ashgate Publishing for agreeing to publish this work, with thanks to Wyndham Thomas, series editor, Heidi Bishop, music editor, and Emma Gallon, editorial assistant.

James Harley
University of Guelph, August 2014

Introduction

In 1969, the year *Kraanerg* was premiered in Ottawa, Canada, composer Iannis Xenakis was featured at the Royan Festival in France, a major venue for contemporary music, with the premiere of a large orchestral work, *Nomos gamma*, where the 100 or so musicians were individually scattered amongst the audience. The festival also presented a new choreography by Maurice Béjart to an existing composition, *Nomos alpha* for solo cello, where the musician performed onstage with a solo dancer. A new work for the Octuor de Paris, *Anaktoria*, was premiered at the Avignon Festival and was subsequently toured around the world, and a large new percussion piece for Les Percussions de Strasbourg, *Persephassa*, was unveiled to much acclaim at the Shiraz Festival in Iran. His research centre, EMAMu, was officially given recognition and support in France that year; and, as he was putting the organization in place, Xenakis was also was in the middle of a five-year sojourn as professor at Indiana University, one of the most important music faculties in the United States. The previous fall of 1968, while working on *Kraanerg* (and teaching in Bloomington), Xenakis was one of four featured composers at the first Journées de Musique Contemporaine in Paris, along with Edgard Varèse, Luciano Berio, and Pierre Henry. On the day devoted to his music, nine works were presented, including orchestral, chamber, choral, and electroacoustic compositions.

By that time, Xenakis was clearly an important figure on the new music scene, in France, the United States, and worldwide. He had only been working as a professional composer, however, for 10 or so years, since being relieved of his duties in the studio of architect Le Corbusier in the fall of 1959. The first significant performance of his music took place in 1955, with the premiere of the orchestral work *Metastaseis* at the Donaueschingen Festival in Germany. Even if we stretch his career to 15 years by 1969, that is still a short time within which to establish oneself as a significant and original voice of the post-World War II era, recognized and celebrated internationally.

Xenakis was ambitious and worked extremely hard, and, given his background as a revolutionary condemned to death by the Greek regime, was not a person to take any aspect of his life for granted, including the fact of his being alive! In a profound sense, he had nothing to lose, and this comes through in his radical approach to music composition. His work with Le Corbusier involved him in large-scale projects that had a major impact on the public. In particular, the Philips Pavilion for the Brussels World Fair in 1958, largely designed by Xenakis himself, engendered a great deal of public and critical attention. He was able to achieve the same kind of impact with his own multimedia projects, beginning with the *Polytope de Montréal* (1967), a large-scale installation for the French Pavilion at that year's World Exposition. His work there was experienced by thousands of visitors, and his *Polytope de Cluny*

(1972), another multimedia event, this time installed in the heart of Paris, reached tens of thousands.

At the same time as Xenakis was exerting himself to produce creative works of significant impact, he developed a body of original theoretical thought that has proven highly influential for not only musicians, but computer scientists and architects as well. His implementation of "stochastic" (random or statistically controlled) procedures has affected the course of computer music, so that such functions are common in all music programming environments. His insights into creating and shaping massed sonorities, complex rhythms, and novel textures have influenced, consciously or not, most composers coming of age in the past half-century. Xenakis has been written into the history books, and by the time of *Kraanerg*, he was well on his way.

This book seeks to highlight Xenakis's work through the spotlight of a single work, *Kraanerg*, produced at an important juncture of his compositional development and professional career. This composition is the largest he ever created, in terms of overall duration, and is a work that crosses disciplines, combining ensemble writing with electronic projection, music with dance and design. Until quite recently, *Kraanerg* was little performed and mostly ignored, a strange fate for such a major work by this composer. We will seek to redress this imbalance in the work's reception by shedding light on the music and the context within which it was composed. We will also provide some background on this fascinating composer, highlighting key features of his music and thought so that the discussion of *Kraanerg* will be meaningful. The recording provided with the book should prove to be a valuable companion to the text, and will hopefully go on to assume primary place in the reader's experience, as the music takes over from the words.

Chapter 1
Biography

The Early Years

Iannis Xenakis was born 29 May 1922 in Brăila, Romania, a port town on the Danube River just upstream from the Black Sea, to Greek parents, Clearchos Xenakis and Photini Pavlou. His father was a successful merchant, and the family – which included two younger brothers, Jason (who became a philosopher in the United States) and Cosmas (who became a painter in Greece) – lived a relatively privileged life amongst the Greek expatriate community. According to Xenakis's biographer, Nouritza Matossian, Photini was an accomplished pianist who played at home for her family and guests, and Clearchos was an opera lover who took occasional trips to attend performances in places like Paris and Bayreuth.[1] In the published interviews with Bálint András Varga, Xenakis mentions hearing Romanian folk music as a child, and being marked by these sounds, ever after associating them with early life experiences.[2]

While the boys were primarily cared for by governesses, as befitting a family of their wealth and social standing, they were nonetheless very close to their mother. It was especially difficult for Iannis and his brothers to lose her to illness when they were still young (Iannis was five or six years old when she died). Her love of music was something that Xenakis held dear and took inspiration from, although it would be more than three decades before he could devote himself to this vocation unreservedly.

At age 10, Xenakis was sent away to boarding school. He spent his school years far away from home on the island of Spetses, located off the Peloponnesian coast in Greece. He resided six years there, and, after suffering through a period of adjustment to boarding school life, went on to excel at both academics and athletics. His love of the sea, which would stay with him throughout his life, was born there at Spetses, with daily swims in the Mediterranean. Françoise Xenakis, his wife, has written of their annual vacation adventures on the sea, primarily around Corsica, where they eventually built a summer home.[3] He became an avid reader, devouring books of fiction (especially science fiction, like Jules Verne), history, and science, with a special love for classical literature and philosophy. Even in Greece, a teenager obsessed with ancient culture, engaging with complex intellectual concepts as

---

[1] Nouritza Matossian, *Xenakis* (London: Kahn & Averill, 1986; first published in French, Paris: Fayard, 1981), 13.

[2] Bálint András Varga, *Conversations with Iannis Xenakis* (London: Faber and Faber, 1996), 10.

[3] Françoise Xenakis, *Moi j'aime pas la mer* (Paris: Balland, 1994).

espoused by Plato, Aristotle, and the others, would have been an unusual fellow, no doubt.

A British headmaster who possessed a gramophone played all kinds of classical music that the boys heard through the open windows of his room, peripherally introducing them to symphonies, concertos, chamber music, etc. Another teacher played piano, and through his open window would have been heard keyboard music by Bach and others. The school had a choir, and sang Palestrina and related repertoire. The students attended a local church on Sundays, where they heard, and would have participated in, the singing particular to Greek Orthodox services. Matossian reports that Xenakis had some piano lessons and studied solfège, but he confessed to being a bad student.[4] That kind of musical study would have been secondary to the focus on reading, academics, and sports. He admitted to Varga that his attraction to music, although extremely powerful, was still nascent, too deeply embedded in his psyche for him to be aware of it enough to act upon.[5]

The commonly understood myth about Xenakis is that he was an outsider (Matossian tells us the name Xenakis means "gentle stranger"), and that he came to music as a neophyte, bringing ideas from mathematics, architecture, and Greek philosophy, with little reference to music traditions, either common practice or modern. While this story is largely true, particularly in the highly original ideas and techniques he would later bring to music composition, a close reading of Xenakis's biography illuminates an early life in which traditional music was present throughout, with an acquisition of skills and knowledge that would have been normal for an educated member of bourgeois European society. What is undeniable is that the young Xenakis showed no particularly outstanding talent or interest in music as a vocation.[6] The desire to devote his life to music would develop later, as we shall see.

Athens

In 1938, after completing his studies at the school in Spetses, Xenakis moved to Athens to prepare for the entrance examination for admittance to the Athens Polytechnic. It took him two years, and three attempts, to be accepted into the engineering program. During that time, along with other studies, Xenakis took piano lessons (briefly), and studied harmony and counterpoint with the Russian-trained Aristotle Koundourov. The cultural life of Athens was not showing at its best during that period, as Greece's government had recently been overthrown and the country placed under a military dictatorship. Nonetheless, Matossian

---

[4] Matossian 1986, 16.
[5] Varga 1996, 13.
[6] It is easy to surmise that Xenakis would have received no encouragement from his father, in spite of his love of opera, as he himself had given up a desire to study theology for a life of commerce in order to help support his eleven younger siblings and then his own family.

reports that Iannis often fell in love, and went on cycling-camping trips to visit archeological sites in the vicinity.[7]

By the time Xenakis was accepted into the Polytechnic in 1940, Hitler's forces had invaded Romania, forcing his father to uproot the family and join him in Athens. Soon after, Mussolini's forces rolled into Greece through Albania, and the war was upon them all. The Polytechnic was only open sporadically through the war years, and it would take Xenakis six years, through great upheaval and deprivation, to complete his degree in civil engineering.

It was during this period that Xenakis was drawn into the Greek Resistance, eventually becoming a student leader and a staunch member of the Communist Party. There was little respite from the struggles and hardships, but one of Xenakis's close friends in the Resistance was a musician who played for him whenever they could find access to a piano. Without necessarily connecting the sonic environment of the war to music, the sounds of demonstrations and warfare nonetheless imprinted themselves deeply on Xenakis's memory, providing later inspiration for elements of his aesthetic expressivity. Xenakis admitted to Varga that during this period in Athens he tried writing melodies to set lines of poetry by Sappho to music.[8] He later returned to this poetic inspiration, in works such as *Psappha* (1975) for solo percussion, and *Aïs* (1980) for voice, percussion, and orchestra.

In December 1944, the Resistance battled valiantly to impede the progress of occupying forces; by this time the Axis armies had been displaced by the British, who ended up supporting the Greek military dictatorship for fear of Communist contagion. During the fighting, Xenakis was seriously injured by mortar fire, taking a piece of shrapnel to the face. He almost died, and ended up losing one eye and gaining a disfiguring scar across the left side of his face. His father managed to get him to a hospital where he was treated and was then obliged to convalesce for three months. When he emerged in March 1945, the fighting was over, but the persecution of Resistance fighters was in full swing. Xenakis returned to his studies, completing his final examinations by summer 1946. He was compelled to enlist in the military, working at a desk job; but at the same time, leftist activists began to be rounded up, and any who did not recant Resistance/Communist allegiances ended up in concentration camps where many were put to death. Xenakis refused to sign a recantation, and as a result went into hiding amongst family acquaintances in Athens. By autumn 1947, he was forced to flee the country, as it seemed only a matter of time until he would be caught and surely killed, if not for being in the Resistance then for deserting his military post.

---

[7] Matossian 1986, 18.
[8] Varga 1996, 14.

New Life in Paris

After a harrowing journey through Italy, aided by contacts in the Communist Party, Xenakis arrived in Paris in November 1947. France was still very much in recovery from the war and Nazi occupation, so Paris, suffering from fuel and food shortages, strikes, and devastation, was not quite the city of light and love as it is usually known. He was traumatized, lonely, exhausted, and poor, with no legitimate papers of identity or residency. Nonetheless, Xenakis had a few Communist and Greek expatriate contacts, and within a few months he found himself working (under the table, one assumes) in the atelier of famed architect Le Corbusier. This situation proved to be a stroke of incredible good fortune and would have far-reaching consequences for Xenakis.

Le Corbusier (1887–1965) is considered one of the most important figures of modern architecture. He had a particular interest in improving living conditions in urban environments, designing and building a number of large-scale projects in cities around the world. His "modulor" system based architectural proportions on human measurements linked to the golden ratio.[9] The period Xenakis worked for him (1947–59) was the most productive of the architect's career. Major projects undertaken during that time included the Unité d'Habitation in Marseilles (1947–52), a large residential complex, and the civic complex of Chandigarh, India (1952–59), a commission involving the design and construction of several major buildings. Xenakis worked on these projects, along with a number of others, his role shifting from engineering assistant to architectural assistant to project manager. His most extensive project involvement was with the Philips Pavilion (1956–58), for which he co-designed the edifice and oversaw construction.

Xenakis's association with Le Corbusier was significant for a couple of reasons. It developed self-confidence, that a master architect would entrust a junior employee with increasing amounts of responsibility and creative, critical input into the work of the atelier. Le Corbusier encouraged discussion, and constantly sought to connect his work to current issues and innovations across a variety of disciplines, including music. This environment would have been highly stimulating for Xenakis, whose creative development in Athens was sublimated by the struggles of the war, occupation, and resistance. Further, Xenakis gained valuable experience managing complex projects, especially the Philips Pavilion, coordinating the various elements, dealing with funders, engineers, technicians, construction contractors, etc. This work would prove him in good stead when he later was able to take on his own large-scale multimedia projects.

With a job in hand, one that not only provided material sustenance but was also creatively and intellectually engaging—and one that might have led Xenakis into a architectural career, had he been more inclined (indeed he continued an active

---

[9] Le Corbusier, *The Modulor* (Basel: Birkhäuser, 1954; first published in French, Boulogne-sur-Seine: Éditions de l'Architecture, 1950).

engagement with the discipline throughout his life)—Xenakis made the decision to embark on a path into music, toward composition. He was not in a position to become a student, full time, but he sought out instruction, eventually arriving on the doorstep of Olivier Messiaen (1908–92), an acclaimed, if non-conformist, composer and a magnetic, dedicated pedagogue. It was not a straightforward path to their acquaintance, though. Meetings with Arthur Honegger and Darius Milhaud at the École Normale were not encouraging, and Nadia Boulanger was unwilling to take him on. Her assistant Annette Dieudonné, however, suggested he approach Messiaen, who accepted auditors into his classes at the Conservatoire (where Xenakis would otherwise never have been accepted as a student due to his lack of traditional training). After meeting him, Messiaen did invite Xenakis to attend his analysis classes (he did not at that time teach composition, officially), which the young man did regularly during the years 1951–53 and occasionally during the following academic year. Other students during those years included Jean Barraqué (France), André Boucourechliev (Bulgaria-France), Michel Decoust (France), Serge Garant (Canada), Betsy Jolas (France), and Karlheinz Stockhausen (Germany).[10] All of them went on to distinguished careers.

The atmosphere *chez* Messiaen was a highly charged one, no doubt, with much attention paid to new music, along with interesting analyses of rhythmic structures in music of various cultures, and much else. In an act of astute insight, the elder composer advised Xenakis to use his own unique gifts—a deep knowledge of Greek culture, experience as an architect, training in advanced mathematics, and a remarkably intense life experience—to create his own music, rather than try to work through the traditional, years-long training in harmony, counterpoint, etc. This bestowal of confidence had a profound effect on the young composer, and his efforts at writing music evolved at an incredible rate.

Early Compositions

The first works Xenakis penned date from 1949, and over the next four years, he wrote quite a collection of short works, 30 or so, primarily for piano or for voice with piano accompaniment. Texts were primarily in Greek, occasionally penned by Xenakis himself. With a few exceptions, these early compositions were unknown for 40 years, at which point composer-musicologist François-Bernard Mâche (also a close friend of the composer) embarked on a study of this music and this formative period of Xenakis's musical life.[11] Subsequently, performers became interested, and a few of these scores have been performed and published. The music that rises above the level of exercise exhibits folkloric elements, looking back to the composer's

---

10   Jean Boivin, *La classe de Messiaen* (Paris: Christian Bourgois, 1995).
11   François-Bernard Mâche, "The Hellenism of Xenakis," *Contemporary Music Review* 8 (1), 1993, 197–211.

Greek and Romanian roots. Certain scores also show a preoccupation with formal, mathematical concerns, including the use of the Fibonacci series. From a Western perspective, the resemblance to the music of Béla Bartók, especially his short works for piano, is unmistakable, although other influences from Greece and elsewhere may also be discernible. While Xenakis was trying to express his identity as a Greek in his music, he was also "coming of age" (musically) in Paris, a hotbed of post-war modernism, in music, art, literature, theater, architecture, and much else. It was also the place where Xenakis met Françoise, the woman who would become his wife in 1953 and with whom he would share the rest of his life. Their daughter Mâkhi was born in 1956.

In 1953, having developed confidence from the generous support of both Le Corbusier and Messiaen, Xenakis embarked on an ambitious composition: it was to be a cycle of three works for voices and orchestra, enacting a kind of ritual called Anastenaria: "a living fragment of past civilizations, which was torn from the destruction of the millenarians by the Greek peasants of Thrace. The cult was established in the age of Constantine the Great, the fourth century A.D., and has been preserved in a primitive state up to our own day."[12] Xenakis wrote texts, created a plan for the whole work, and by May 1953 had completed the first part, *Procession vers les eaux claires*, scored for orchestra with both mixed and male choirs. The piece lasts just 8 minutes, but it is by far the most ambitious work he had undertaken to date. By the end of July that year, he had completed *Le Sacrifice*, the second part of the cycle. The music, however, veered away from the original plan. This piece is scored for orchestra alone, and is highly organized in ways that owe much to the "modal" serialism of Messiaen (where the 12 pitches are ordered from low to high), as in his *Modes de valeurs et d'intensités* from 1949. There is little in this highly abstract study in formalism to connect it to the Dionysian rituals of the Anastenaria, aside from the title. The third part of the cycle was completely abandoned, as Xenakis turned his attention to abstraction and sonority. *Metastaseis*, completed in 1954, is sometimes considered the third piece of the cycle but it is in fact a completely independent work. The first two remained unpublished and unperformed until many decades later, while the latter piece became Xenakis's breakthrough work, launching his career and reputation.

Breakthroughs

The German-born conductor Hermann Scherchen (1891–1966) became a third mentor to Xenakis, along with Le Corbusier and Messiaen. Scherchen was in Paris in 1954 to conduct the premiere of *Déserts* by Edgard Varèse. By the fall of 1954, Xenakis had been accepted as a researcher into the studios of Pierre Schaeffer, now known as the Groupe de Recherches Musicales (GRM), housed within the facilities

---

[12] Mâche 1993, 202.

of Radio France (then known as ORTF) in Paris. This organization was one of the first, and most influential, centers for electronic, or studio-based, music composition in the world. Schaeffer's musical assistant, composer Pierre Henry, was working with Varèse on the production of the tape parts for *Déserts*, and with Varèse and Scherchen for the rehearsals. This composition by Varèse was one of the first ever to combine an ensemble of instrumental musicians with pre-recorded tape interjections. Henry, who had a copy of Xenakis's score *Le Sacrifice* (part of Xenakis's application portfolio for admittance to GRM), passed it along to Scherchen, who declared a willingness to meet the young composer. He ended up expressing that he had no interest in the score that was presented to him, but when Xenakis showed him the new work he was just completing, Scherchen's attention was piqued.[13] *Metastaseis* was unique for the time, with all the strings of the symphony orchestra being scored individually, each part in the opening section being notated as a slow glissando (sliding-note) contour, altogether creating a composite texture that had never been heard in music before. Scherchen discerned the originality in this music, and his support did much to shift the novice composer into the professional realm. Scherchen subsequently conducted many of Xenakis's works, and premiered *Terretektorh*, for spatialized symphony orchestra, at the Royan Festival in 1966, not long before he died.

Acting out of the confidence shown him by Messiaen and Scherchen, Xenakis sent his score for *Metastaseis* to Heinrich Strobel, director of the Donaueschingen Festival in Germany, and the work was premiered at the festival in October 1955, with Hans Rosbaud conducting the SudWestFunk Radio Orchestra. The performance provoked a scandal, not so much because the music was radical (Donaueschingen was a major festival of contemporary music, after all), but because it did not conform to the prevailing serialist aesthetic. To put Xenakis's reception into context, *Le marteau sans maître* by Pierre Boulez—a sophisticated new work by one of the central, and most polemic, figures of the serialist movement—was premiered at the same festival, to great acclaim. Regardless of critical reception by the new music elite (who somehow overlooked the intricate serial structure of the central section of the score), the glissando textures and other massed effects of *Metastaseis* made a strong impression on many who heard it, and Xenakis became a composer to watch, virtually overnight.

At the same time, Xenakis had enough assurance to begin writing about his new approach to music and his thoughts on the limitations of prevailing trends: his article "The crisis of serial music" was published in 1955.[14] Scherchen encouraged him to articulate his ideas, and published many of the composer's early articles, including that first incendiary one, in his journal, *Gravesaner Blätter*, between 1955 and 1966. A collection of these articles was published in French in 1963 as *Musiques formelles*,

---

[13] Matossian 1986, 78.
[14] "La crise de la musique sérielle." This article was reprinted, in French, in 1994: Iannis Xenakis, *Kéleütha: Ecrits* (Paris: L'Arche), 39–43.

then in English with additional material in 1971 as *Formalized Music* (updated again in 1992).[15]

The opportunity Scherchen provided Xenakis to formulate and communicate his original approach to music proved invaluable, and no doubt facilitated his rapid development as a composer. One of the criticisms he leveled at the serialist approach was that in complex textures, it is virtually impossible to perceive the row structures (of pitch, duration, etc.). The music in effect is statistical in spite of the elaborate generative techniques. His background in engineering and continuing interest in advanced mathematics led him to propose an alternative, based on probability functions. Whereas such functions are used in engineering to calculate a variety of factors important in construction, Xenakis turned the functions around to create rather than to analyze. He called this technique "stochastics," and he applied it extensively in his next composition, completed in 1956. *Pithoprakta*, a second work for orchestra featuring divisi strings like *Metastaseis*, is nonetheless quite different from the earlier score. The main features of the work are the complex textures that form "clouds" of sound, where one perceives the global characteristics but rarely the individual details. In a texture of plucked sounds in the strings, for example, one can sense the registers and ambitus of the notes as a whole, along with changes of dynamics and density. Xenakis used different subdivisions of the beat for each instrument so that there could be no perception of rhythm in the traditional sense, only statistical sensations of rhythmic textures (with occasional exceptions for contrast). The attack points (placement in time) of each pizzicato event, and the pitch of each event, were calculated using stochastic functions, essentially a process of random selection, as noted in the Introduction, with a certain degree of control over input settings for the mathematical routines.

In addition to deploying new compositional techniques for creating complex textures, Xenakis exhibited a great deal of imagination in his treatment of the strings, calling for the players to knock percussively on the body of their instruments, tap the strings with the wood of the bow, pluck pizzicato-glissandi, etc. In fact, there are 21 different textures presented in *Pithoprakta* (counting silence, here treated as an integral element of the music), heard in succession or in layers.[16] It is a fascinating soundworld that he created, one not heard before (such texture-based orchestral music by composers such as György Ligeti and Krzysztof Penderecki would not appear until a few years later). Scherchen conducted the premiere of *Pithoprakta* in 1957 at the Musica Viva Festival in Munich. Both *Metastaseis* and *Pithoprakta* were broadcast in Germany and elsewhere, and may well have been heard by composers such as Ligeti and Penderecki, who were developing their own compositional styles around that time.

---

[15] Iannis Xenakis, *Formalized Music*, revised edition (Hillsdale, NY: Pendragon, 1992; first published in English, Bloomington: Indiana University Press, 1971; first published in French, Paris: La Revue Musicale/Richard-Masse, 1963).

[16] James Harley, *Xenakis: His Life in Music* (New York: Routledge, 2004), 15.

While Xenakis was working on these scores and writing articles on his original approach to composition, he was still working full time for Le Corbusier. He was also spending time at GRM, learning studio production techniques, and creating his first electroacoustic composition, *Diamorphoses*, completed in 1957. In the period 1956–58 he served as project manager for the design and construction of the Philips Pavilion for the World Fair in Brussels, as noted in the Introduction. Le Corbusier was often absent, working on his large civic project in Chandigarh, India, so Xenakis assumed a great deal of responsibility for the pavilion. Working from initial floor-plan sketches provided by Le Corbusier, he created a design of intersecting hyperbolic paraboloids, essentially collapsing the distinction between wall and ceiling. He also liaised with the engineers on producing thin reinforced concrete sheets that would conform to the curving surfaces of the design so that it could be entirely self-supporting. In addition, he worked with the audio engineers of the Philips Corporation, who designed a unique sound system for the pavilion that comprised 425 loudspeakers distributed throughout the pavilion, with custom routing technology for diffusing sound along pre-configured paths of loudspeakers. They also installed lighting and projection equipment for *Le poème électronique*, a multimedia presentation within the pavilion conceived by Le Corbusier in collaboration with composer Edgard Varèse, filmmaker Philippe Agostini, and graphic designer Jean Petit. Xenakis was asked to compose a short electronic music interlude to be played as the public entered and departed the pavilion. While the original multimedia presentation did not survive the pavilion (which was destroyed after the World Fair closed in fall 1958), both Varèse's *Le poème électronique* and Xenakis's *Concret PH* survive as classics of electroacoustic creation.[17]

The Composer's Life

Xenakis was released from Le Corbusier's employ in September 1959. The primary reason was the conflict created by the young assistant demanding credit for the design of the Philips Pavilion. Such audacity was unheard of in architectural studios, and is another measure of Xenakis's soaring self-confidence through this period. It is worth noting that Le Corbusier did in fact grant Xenakis co-authorship of the pavilion, but it must have seemed apparent that it was time to move on. Xenakis took the occasion to finally commit himself to music (although he continued to do freelance engineering work on the side, to help support his family until his professional career as a composer was more established). By that time—in addition to the orchestral works *Metastaseis* and *Pithoprakta*, and the electroacoustic works *Diamorphoses* and *Concret PH*—he had composed *Achorripsis* for chamber orchestra (premiered

---

[17] A virtual-reality reconstruction of the original presentation has been produced more recently, described in Vincenzo Lombardo et al., "A virtual-reality reconstruction of *Poème électronique* based on philological research," *Computer Music Journal* 33 (2), 2009, 24–47.

by Scherchen in Buenos Aires); *Analogique A & B* for string ensemble and studio-produced electronic sounds (again premiered by Scherchen, in Switzerland); *Syrmos* for string ensemble (not premiered until 1965, by Constantin Simonovitch); and *Duel* for two orchestras (not premiered until much later, 1971). This latter work applied "game theory" to music where the two conductors are instructed to choose which section of music to play in response to what the other chooses to play, guided by stochastically derived numerical scores attached to each decision. Where other composers by that time were allowing performers freedom to choose the order of sections of a piece, and freedom over other aspects of the music (such as in Stockhausen's *Klavierstücke XI* from 1956), Xenakis held to mathematical principles to guide such freedoms. He wrote a second such work, *Stratégie*, in 1962, which by good fortune was premiered at the Venice Biennale that year, conducted by Bruno Maderna and Constantin Simonovitch.

This list of works, all completed within three years while still working for Le Corbusier, indicates how hard Xenakis was prepared to work to achieve his dream of devoting his life to music. In his conversations with Varga, he speaks to a motivation that comes from barely escaping death earlier in his life: "For years I was tormented by guilt at having left the country for which I'd fought. I left my friends—some were in prison, others were dead … I felt I had a mission. I had to do something important to regain the right to live."[18] He had been given a new life, and did not want to waste it, or take it for granted. While this driving force may have helped him find the energy to devote himself to his creative pursuits, it may also have reinforced his courage to continually strive for originality and expressive force.

At the same time, the sudden shift to life as a freelance composer meant Xenakis needed to find work. In 1960–61, he produced soundtracks for three short documentary films, through his association with GRM. Two of them, primarily scored for instruments, were not heard beyond the distribution of the films, and the scores were not published.[19] His music for the third film, *Orient-Occident*, by director Enrico Fulchignoni, was electroacoustic, and Xenakis was able to create a concert version that has been widely presented and heard.[20] In 1962, Xenakis produced one final electroacoustic work at GRM, *Bohor*, for eight channels (before eight-track tape recorders were widely available). This unrelentingly noisy work

---

[18] Varga 1996, 47.

[19] One of these films, *Vasarely*, was recently uncovered, and has been issued on Mode Records with the music that Xenakis created for it (Mode Records 203, 2008). This 8-minute film is based on an exhibition of "cinétique" works by the visual artist Victor Vasarely. While Xenakis may not have considered his instrumental score for this film to be worth preserving, he was sufficiently impressed by Vasarely's work that he later approached him to do the set and costume design for *Kraanerg*.

[20] Details about this film and Xenakis's production of the music for it have recently been uncovered at the Xenakis Archives. See Makis Solomos, "*Orient-Occident*: From the film version to the concert version," in *Iannis Xenakis: Das elektroakustische Werk*, Ralph Paland and Christoph von Blumröder, editors (Vienna: Apfel, 2009), 118–31.

provoked another scandal for the composer—Pierre Schaeffer, founder and guiding force of GRM, had an intensely negative reaction to it. After that, Xenakis's ongoing association with GRM as one of its primary associate composers wound down, and he had only sporadic visits to the studio for specific projects from that point on. He also chose to no longer pursue employment as a film composer, perhaps because of the constraints on creative freedom such collaborations generally impose on the composer (given that the director is usually the one in charge). Nonetheless, Xenakis seems to have retained from his experiences at GRM a technical facility in the studio and the ability to oversee recordings of instrumental ensembles. These would be valuable skills that he would draw on for later work, and for *Kraanerg* in particular.

Xenakis also pursued opportunities to score incidental music for the theater, in particular stage works based on the Greek classics he had devoured as a boy. The first such opportunity came in 1964, when Greek stage director Alexis Solomos invited Xenakis to compose music for a production of Aeschylus's *The Suppliants*, for presentation in the ancient amphitheater at Epidaurus, Greece. The composer himself, still in exile with a death warrant on his head by the continuing military regime in Athens, was not able to attend the rehearsals or performances. But, it was an important project for him, one that enabled him to return, creatively at least, to his origins. In addition to providing instrumental musical interludes, Xenakis set the choruses to music, adopting an archaic, quasi-modal style that followed the rhythmic scansion of the text closely. He created complex sonic textures by having the singers of the chorus also play various hand-percussion instruments, improvising on cue to conjure atmospheric "clouds" of sound. With the exception of *Polla ta Dhina* (1962), a work primarily for orchestra with a children's chorus chanting a Greek text on a single note, this was the first work to engage with text since Xenakis's early efforts in the years prior to *Metastaseis*. Xenakis collaborated with Solomos again, on *Oresteïa* (1966), for a theater festival in the USA. In 1967, he worked with French director Jean-Louis Barrault on a production of *Medea* (a Latin text by Seneca, nonetheless setting a Greek story). Thereafter, Xenakis chose to concentrate on projects where he retained full creative control. He was only enticed back into the theater to do incidental music once more much later, in 1993, by David Freeman of London Opera Factory, for a production of *The Bacchae* by Euripides. Nonetheless, he did produce concert versions of his three early theater works, and the suite for *Oresteïa* has taken on a life of its own, engendering theatrical productions of various kinds based on his concert suite. Xenakis added two more pieces featuring a solo voice to *Oresteïa* for productions in 1987 and 1992.

Movement and "Spéctacle"

While Xenakis thereafter eschewed incidental music, he did not avoid the theater, as we shall see with *Kraanerg*. Rather, he became more interested in exploring the

Figure 1.1   Iannis Xenakis, c. 1968 (Gilbert Rancy, photographer, Xenakis Archives, Bibliothèque nationale de France).

theatrical potential of abstract music. He did this in two main ways. In the first, he sought to spatialize sound, including instrumental music. In the second, he sought to integrate the music into multimedia presentations involving sound, lights, design, and architecture. After his experimental "game theory" works for two orchestras separated on stage (*Duel*, *Stratégie*), Xenakis's first instrumental work to explore spatialization was *Eonta*, a chamber work for piano and five brass from 1964. The music for piano is quite sharply differentiated from the brass material, and the contrast is emphasized by having the brass players move around on stage while the pianist remains fixed in position. The trumpet and trombone are highly directional instruments, so when the instruments are pointed away from the audience, the changes of both timbre and dynamics are highly distinct. Xenakis has the players change positions, change directions while in one position, play directly into the body of the piano (to create a resonance effect), and, in one remarkable passage, move "stochastically" (unpredictably) around the stage while playing (and all the while avoiding the other players).

While the sonic effects of the spatialization are notable, the choreography also makes for engaging "theater." Xenakis carried these experiments further in two works for orchestra: *Terretektorh* (1966) and *Nomos gamma* (1969). For both these works, the individual musicians are distributed throughout the hall (an ordinary concert hall would not do for these works, clearly), with the audience seated amongst them. The music comes from all around the listeners, but each one hears a different mix in terms of balance and location. In *Terretektorh*, each musician is also required to play hand percussion and sirens, producing massed sonic effects (as in *The Suppliants*) that complement the more linear textures of the orchestral music. In *Nomos gamma*, Xenakis deploys eight dedicated percussionists around the perimeter of the performing area, and he then continues to explore the possibilities for moving sounds around the audience in *Persephassa* (1969) for six percussionists, which places the audience in the middle of the ring of performers.

Building on his experiences of Le Corbusier's *Poème électronique*—with its combination of spatialized electronic music, lights, film, sculpture, and architectural design—Xenakis embarked on his first self-authored multimedia project in 1967. The *Polytope de Montréal* was commissioned for the French Pavilion of the World Expo in Montreal, Canada. Xenakis was given the large atrium space of the pavilion to create an installation. He created a kinetic design from steel cables stretching from top to bottom, and a light show, to run in tandem with a musical score for four ensembles (in the event, a recording was used rather than live musicians, presented from a four-channel tape with loudspeakers located to give a similar effect of directionality). The 6-minute presentation of spatialized music and lights was repeated many times a day, and many thousands of visitors experienced it over the months of the World Expo. Xenakis coined the term "polytope" to describe such multimedia presentations, and he went on to produce a number of others: *Persepolis* (1971) for the Shiraz Festival, Iran; *Polytope de Cluny* (1972) for the historic Roman baths in Paris; *Polytope de Mycènes* (1978) for Mycenae, Greece; and *Le Diatope: La Légende d'Eer* (1978) for the opening of the Centre Pompidou, Paris (also presented in Bonn, Germany). For this last production, Xenakis was able to design and create the pavilion for his 45-minute presentation of spatialized music, lights (including lasers), and text (printed in the program booklet rather than presented audibly). This was a new kind of theater, multi-sensorial and immersive.

International Reputation

Throughout this period of remarkable compositional activity (a pace which continued for decades, until illness finally slowed him down), Xenakis began to travel a great deal, giving lectures and presenting concerts. He had no experience as a performer, so he did not conduct, as composers such as Igor Stravinsky or Pierre Boulez have done. But, his ideas were new, and people the world over were interested in hearing what he had to say, both in his music and through his words. In 1961, he was invited to Tokyo to participate in a conference, "East-West Music Encounter." Other occidental composers in attendance there included Luciano Berio and Elliott Carter. Most significant for Xenakis were his encounters with Asian musicians, with whom he would develop life-long friendships and associations. These included composer-pianist Yuji Takahashi, composer Toru Takemitsu, conductor Seiji Ozawa, and Philippine composer-ethnomusicologist José Maceda (who invited Xenakis to Manila to an international conference/festival in 1966 where Maceda also conducted *Achorripsis*). The year following Xenakis's first trip to Japan, Takahashi premiered a new solo piano work, *Herma*, in Tokyo, then traveled to Paris to perform the solo piano part for the premiere of *Eonta* in 1964. Ozawa (with second conductor Hiroshi Wakasugi) presented the Japanese premiere of *Stratégie* in 1966. Xenakis returned to Japan in 1970 to create a 12-channel electroacoustic work, *Hibiki-Hana-Ma*, for the World Fair in Osaka. In 1985, he composed a work for traditional Japanese instruments, *Nyuyo*. Later, in 1990, he wrote a short orchestral score, *Tuorakemsu*, to celebrate Takemitsu's sixtieth birthday. Still later, in 1997, he returned to Japan to accept the prestigious Kyoto Prize.

In 1963, American composer Aaron Copland invited Xenakis to the Tanglewood Summer Music Festival to teach composition (Copland later conducted the US premiere of *Pithoprakta* in San Francisco). This was the first of several trips to North America over the next few years, culminating in the appointment to a professorship at Indiana University in 1967. Just after his sojourn at Tanglewood, however, Xenakis took up a one-year residency in Berlin through the Ford Foundation. While this residency did not curtail his activities, it did provide, for the first time, a base of support for his work that enabled him to focus on his music and writings. The freelance engineering work to pay some of the family bills was put aside at last.

Back in Paris, conductor Constantin Simonovitch organized the first Xenakis monograph concert, which took place at the Salle Gaveau in May 1965. Yuji Takahashi returned, to perform *Herma* and the piano part of *Eonta*, and the other works presented were: *ST/10* (1962) for mixed ensemble; *Analogique A & B* (1958–59) for string ensemble and electronic sounds; *Syrmos* (1959) for string ensemble; *Atrées* (1962) for mixed ensemble; and *Achorripsis* (1957) for chamber orchestra. This ambitious program, received not without controversy,[21] marked Xenakis's arrival as a significant musical voice in France (and the world). This acknowledgment was aided by the awarding of the Grand Prix de l'Académie du Disque Français for the Chant du Monde recording of *Metastaseis*, *Pithoprakta*, and *Eonta*, the first monograph album issued of Xenakis's music. Many more such concerts, recordings, and awards would follow. In November–December 1977, 18 concerts entirely devoted to Xenakis were presented in and around Paris, a *Cycle Xenakis*, culminating with the premiere of *Jonchaies*, a major orchestral work performed by the Orchestre National de France, conducted by Michel Tabachnik.

---

[21] Xenakis's music was like no one else's; he continued to be perceived as an "outsider" by some critics.

Chapter 2
Musical Background to *Kraanerg*

Formalization

In the mid-1950s, as Xenakis began to develop his compositional strategies in earnest, encouraged by Scherchen and Messiaen, he embarked on a process of "formalization." That is, he started piecing together a theory of music, first articulated in the series of articles he wrote for *Gravesaner Blätter* and culminating in the publication of *Formalized Music*. As his point of departure, he decided to take nothing for granted, to question everything. As a result, he outlined what he called the "fundamental phases of a musical work."[1] These phases can be summarized as follows:

1. Initial conceptions.
2. Definition of the sonic entities.
3. Definition of the transformations.
4. Microcomposition.
5. Sequential programming.
6. Implementation of calculations.
7. Final symbolic result.
8. Sonic realization.

While this schematic outline of the compositional process may seem perhaps overly formal (an impression heightened by the composer's algebraic formulations for most of the phases), there are some significant features that should be noted. The first phase, "initial conceptions," acknowledges the primary role of intuition. The composer's imagination might give rise to the idea of creating music based on intersticed string glissandi (as in *Metastaseis*) or stochastic clouds of different types of discrete sounds (as in *Pithoprakta*). The notion of "sonic entities" is also of critical importance. In his discussion in *Formalized Music*, Xenakis states that "the sonic entities of the classical orchestra can be represented in a first approximation ... of four usually independent variables": timbre or instrumental family; pitch; intensity, or dynamic form; and duration.[2]

It is crucial for understanding Xenakis's music to realize that pitch is not privileged, but bundled with these other sonic parameters. Until that point in musical history, virtually all concert music treated pitch as the primary element of composition. Edgard Varèse is an exception, with his attention to percussion and

---

[1] Xenakis 1992, 22.
[2] Xenakis 1992, 23.

sonority; he was an important influence for Xenakis.[3] It is also significant that "transformations" of the sonic entities are considered fundamental. This phase comprises the macrocomposition of the work: "general choice of logical framework, i.e., of the elementary algebraic operations and the setting up of relations between entities, sets, and their symbols ... and the arrangement of these operations in lexicographic time with the aid of succession and simultaneity."[4]

As Xenakis admits, "the order of this list [of fundamental phases] is not really rigid. Permutations are possible in the course of the working out of a composition. Most of the time, these phases are unconscious and defective."[5] As we shall see with *Kraanerg*, Xenakis was very willing to be flexible in working out the music within the framework of a theoretical foundation or plan. For his first "formalized" project, though, he applied his rules quite rigidly.

Achorripsis, for 21 instruments, was completed in 1957. Part of the "initial conceptions" for this work was to seek "the greatest possible *asymmetry* ... and the *minimum of constraints, causality, and rules*."[6] To this end, Xenakis applied stochastic procedures to a number of aspects of the music, most particularly in the microcomposition phase. He defined seven instrumental groups or playing modes: piccolo/clarinets; oboe/bassoons; string glissando; percussion; string pizzicato; brass; string arco. The "transformations" were randomized by removing any link from one event to another. On the global level, the composer defined 28 sections, each lasting 15 seconds. A mean density of events per section was determined for each of the seven instrumental/timbral entities, the densities being selected from a "scale" of events per measure: 0, 5, 10, 15, 20. Further stochastic procedures were applied to fix particular events within each section, including the selection of pitches, durations, and dynamic levels/forms.[7] The only constraints for pitches were the registral limits of each instrument; the attack points and durations for events within sections were also randomized, although guided by the global density settings, with bars/beats subdivided differently (into threes, fours, and fives) for selected instruments in order to avoid a perception of pulse. The dynamic levels were applied not to individual notes but to sections, and to instrument groups over individual instruments. This helped to further delineate the timbral groups one from another when they are sounding together in a particular section of the piece. For the listener, there is no sense in trying to follow the succession of pitches, intervals, and harmonic aggregates, as there are no such organized structures to be perceived. Instead, one can follow the changing densities of activity and instrumental color. *Achorripsis*

---

[3] As noted in Chapter 1, Xenakis met Varèse in 1954. He also had contact with him in 1958, when they both were involved in Le Corbusier's *Poème électronique* project for the Philips Pavilion.
[4] Xenakis 1992, 22.
[5] Xenakis 1992, 22.
[6] Xenakis 1992, 23.
[7] Dynamic forms referring here to crescendos, decrescendos, etc.

is rather like a kaleidoscope in sound, built from ever-shifting combinations of a limited set of sonic entities, with individual events passing by with little significance in themselves. While Xenakis went on to develop additional tools (for organizing pitch structures, for example), this kaleidoscopic conception of musical form would remain fundamental to his compositional aesthetic, and would be given its grandest expression in the 75 minutes of *Kraanerg*.

Achorripsis was a success. Scherchen premiered it in Buenos Aires in 1958 and conducted it elsewhere. Other conductors such as Simonovitch and Maceda took it up, and it was released on disc in 1969. Interestingly, while the compositional approach is radically different from the serialist music that was prevalent at the time, *Achorripsis* does not sound radically different. The similarity is undoubtedly due to the pointillistic textures, the global sonorities being built from discrete events. This similarity would also support Xenakis's argument that the perception of complex serial structures occurs statistically rather than linearly. *Achorripsis* proves his point by being generated statistically to achieve a similar result. It is worth noting that, by this time, John Cage was composing similarly pointillistic scores using "chance procedures." His approach did not incorporate the advanced mathematics of probability functions, but he nonetheless developed a sophisticated methodology for applying chance to music.[8]

Computer Algorithms

The elaborate mathematical procedures Xenakis carried out to determine the many hundreds, even thousands, of details in scores like *Achorripsis* or *Pithoprakta* were extremely time-consuming. Even in the early days of computer technology, he could see the efficacy of harnessing the processing power of a digital calculating machine to assist him in his compositional work. Along with everything else he was doing, Xenakis began to teach himself the FORTRAN computer programming language and to implement his "fundamental phases" as a computer algorithm. In order to do this, he was required to fix the details of the process precisely, as he did not need to do when working by hand/intuition. He essentially adapted the approach he took in composing *Achorripsis*, as outlined below:

---

[8] For references to Cage's work, see: Kostas Paparrigopoulos, "Western and Eastern approach of chance in the music of Xenakis and Cage: Theses and contra-theses," in *International Symposium Iannis Xenakis, Athens, May 2005, Definitive Proceedings*, Makis Solomos, Anastasia Georgaki, and Giorgos Zervos, editors (2006, http://cicm.mshparisnord.org/ColloqueXenakis/papers/Paparrigopoulos.pdf); James Pritchett, *The Music of John Cage* (Cambridge: Cambridge University Press, 1996).

1. The work consists of a succession of sequences or movements (their durations are independent).
2. Definition of the mean density of the sounds during each sequence or movement.
3. Composition of the orchestra (sonic entities) during each sequence or movement.
4. Definition of the moment of the occurrence of each sound within each sequence or movement.
5. Attribution to each sound of an instrument drawn from the orchestra (sonic entities).
6. Attribution of a pitch as a function of the assigned instrument.
7. Attribution of a glissando speed if the sonic entity is characterized as a glissando.
8. Attribution of a duration to the sounds emitted.
9. Attribution of dynamic forms to the sounds emitted.[9]

It is significant that his "initial conceptions" are limited to the determination of a number of sequences (or movements) and their durations (the sections not being fixed as in the earlier work), along with a mean density for each. His algorithm also implies that the instrumentation will be divided into a number of groups, or sonic entities, as in *Achorripsis*. For this project, at least, Xenakis understood musical form as a succession of segments, contrasting in density and sonic entity. The details, like pitch and rhythm, are calculated stochastically and are not embedded in any larger-scale organizational structure. They are secondary elements in Xenakis's conception of music, and this is one of the most radical aspects of his work at that time.

It is worth recalling that in the late 1950s/early 1960s, when Xenakis was working out his algorithms to run on a computer, there was no easy access to digital technology. It is likely that there would have been just one computer in Paris, housed at the offices of IBM-France. Access to such a facility would have been difficult (and likely expensive), as IBM's main business model at that time was to provide access to expertise and technology, not to sell computers. Therefore, a fledgling, independent programmer would have had little opportunity to troubleshoot, necessitating an extremely methodical, careful approach to writing the code. Xenakis made the acquaintance of a computer engineer, François Genuys, who worked for IBM at the time. Genuys provided guidance and also facilitated access to the computer (he went on to become a collaborator at the EMAMu research facility Xenakis set up later).

The directors of IBM-France were no doubt intrigued by the novel idea of making music with a computer. There had been pioneering work in computer music carried out in the United States beginning in 1956. Lejaren Hiller (with Leonard Isaacson) at the University of Illinois, Urbana-Champaign, had developed algorithms for generating compositional data (his *Illiac Suite* for string quartet was completed in

---

[9] Xenakis 1992, 134–43.

1957). By 1957, Max Mathews, an engineer at Bell Laboratories, had developed the first program for digital sound synthesis.[10] There was a great deal of public attention given to the newly developing digital technology at that time, including much debate about machine intelligence and creativity. The idea of music being created by computer fed right into this discussion. Xenakis was less interested in the issues stirring the public than in the utility of taking advantage of the computer's processing power to aid his own work. Nonetheless, he was able to wax poetical about the potential of the digital age:

> With the aid of electronic computers the composer becomes a sort of pilot: he presses the buttons, introduces coordinates, and supervises the controls of a cosmic vessel sailing in the space of sound, across sonic constellations and galaxies that he could formerly glimpse only as a distant dream.[11]

Records indicate that IBM-France granted Xenakis access to the computer on four occasions in 1962, the resulting data being used to produce a family of works: *ST/10* for 10 instruments; *ST/4* for string quartet (an adaptation of *ST/10*); *ST/48* for orchestra; *Morsima-Amorsima* for four instruments; and *Atrées* for 11 instruments (another short work, *Amorsima-Morsima*, for 10 instruments, was withdrawn from the composer's catalogue). On 24 May 1962, the company opened its doors to invited members of the public for an on-site concert of two of these works, *ST/10* and *ST/4*. This event certainly increased Xenakis's notoriety, but it also helped to convince him of the value of digital technology. This conviction, and his collaboration/friendship with Genuys, led him to work to establish a research centre, EMAMu (Équipe de Mathématique et d'Automatique Musicales), which was established in 1966, and obtained funding and facilities in 1969. EMAMu became CEMAMu (Centre d'Études de Mathématique et Automatique Musicales) in 1972, and continued its work until Xenakis's death in 2001. He continued to work with computers for a wide variety of tasks—from algorithmic composition to sound synthesis to programmable lighting and multimedia to graphic-audio interfacing—throughout his life. He is considered one of the important pioneers in the field of computer music.[12]

---

[10] Digital-to-analog converter technology, needed to turn computer-generated data into sound, was extremely rare at that time, possibly only found at Bell Labs.
[11] Xenakis 1992, 144.
[12] See James Harley, "Computational approaches to composition of notated instrumental music: Xenakis and other pioneers," in *The Oxford Handbook of Computer Music*, Roger Dean, editor (Oxford: Oxford University Press, 2009), 109–32.

Other Formal Models: Sieves and Groups

Xenakis's *ST* pieces are all similar in their basic conception: sections delineated by overall density and combinations of sonic entities; randomized selection of pitch and rhythm. He had already begun, however, to explore other conceptions of musical form. In *Analogique A & B* (1958–59) he implemented a form of memory (Markov chains), whereby the selection of pitches (and other parameters such as durations and dynamics) would be stochastic but constrained by prior selections. In *Herma* (1961) and *Eonta* (1963), he utilized large pitch collections, whereby stochastic processes would draw from the elements of these collections. The deployment in time of these collections constitutes an important structural element of the music. In the period 1963–66, Xenakis went on to formulate two important theoretical axioms that would greatly enrich his compositional approach: 1) sieve theory; 2) group theory. The latter proved especially important for *Kraanerg*.

The application of stochastics to music provided an efficient way to generate surface complexity, but Xenakis came to realize that the ordering of specific events or details could also be a useful compositional strategy. After all, in architecture (and most music), the overall form and specific design details are not generated using random processes; they are fixed, and the formal organization is allied with structural relationships and necessities. His search for a theoretical basis for the deterministic elements of music led him to ancient Greek thought. Study of Byzantine theory regarding scales and intervals helped Xenakis arrive at a fundamental realization: that music could be thought of as containing "outside time" and "inside time" elements.[13] Different organizational principles can be applied for each category. A primary example of "outside time" elements can be found in pitch structures like modes. A mode can govern the organization of a musical work, but the specific intervallic relationships that characterize the mode exist independently of the music; the musical surface does not usually present an ordered exposition of the mode, the intervallic relationships inherent to the mode are realized cumulatively as the music unfolds. In other words, the mode exists "outside time." Xenakis then went on to develop his own approach to creating modes, or, more generally, arithmetical ordered sets of values. These "sieves," as he called them, could be applied to pitch, rhythm (duration), and other parameters. He used algebraic procedures to create these ordered interval sets, accommodating the possibility to have cyclical repetitions (or not). In *Formalized Music* Xenakis uses this sieve procedure to demonstrate how to mathematically generate a major scale, an ordered set that has asymmetries as well as repetitions (at the octave, or 12-step cycle).[14] His major scale derivation is summarized in Table 2.1.

The "period" indicates the number of steps of a repeating pattern; "modulus" indicates a smaller grouping of the period based on a divisor (here, 3 or 4);

---

[13] Xenakis 1992, 180–94.
[14] Xenakis 1992, 209–10.

Table 2.1 Sieve-based derivation of major scale

Period (12)	0	1	2	3	4	5	6	7	8	9	10	11	12 (0)
Modulus 3(tr2)			x			x			x			x	
Complement 3(tr2)	x	x		x	x		x	x	x	x	x		x
Mod 4(tr0)	x				x				x				x
Intersection A	x				x								x
Mod 3(tr1)		x			x			x			x		
Comp 3(tr1)	x	x	x	x		x	x		x	x		x	x
Mod 4(tr1)						x				x			
Intersection B						x				x			
Union A+B	x				x	x				x			x
Mod 3(tr2)			x			x			x			x	
Mod 4(tr2)			x				x				x		
Intersection C			x										
Union A+B+C	x		x		x	x				x			x
Mod 3(tr0)	x			x			x			x			x
Comp 3(tr0)		x	x	x	x	x			x	x		x	x
Mod 4(tr3)									x			x	
Intersection D									x			x	
Union A+B+C+D	x		x		x	x			x	x		x	x
	C		D		E	F		G		A		B	C

"transposition" (tr) indicates that the modulus markers can be moved along the steps of the sieve rather than beginning at the starting point (0); "complement" indicates the steps that are not defined by the related modulus operation; "intersection" indicates the steps that are common to two or more defined operations; "union" indicates the gathering of all steps defined by two or more operations. Table 2.1 outlines the operations and groupings of operations that enabled Xenakis to define a periodic sieve that is equivalent to a traditional scale. For his own music, he created unique sieves to work with.

Xenakis also proposed "metabolae," transformations of the sieves by systematic manipulation of their operational elements (e.g., altering the period divisors from 3 and 4 to 2 and 6). The results of such transformations are mathematically related but the intervallic connections between the sieves may be less apparent to our ears. Nonetheless, metabolae provided Xenakis with a rich source of ordered-set families that could be applied to pitch organization, rhythmic patterns, and so forth.

The first work Xenakis composed using sieve theory techniques was *Nomos alpha* (1966) for solo cello. He discusses this piece in detail in *Formalized Music*, and this exposition in fact represents the composer's most detailed analysis of any of his own works.[15] He likely considered it significant because of being the first rigorous application of sieve theory and also group theory techniques. This was the period when Xenakis was deeply concerned with theoretical matters, and was writing the articles that would form the basis for his most significant publication, *Formalized Music* (a French version was published in 1963, as *Musiques formelles*, but he expanded it considerably for the 1971 Indiana University Press publication in English). In subsequent years, and for the rest of his career, he was much more concerned with the creative application of his theoretical work. The largest exception to this stance was the work he devoted to preparing a doctoral thesis for the Université de Paris I (Sorbonne), which he defended in 1976.[16]

Where sieve theory enabled ordered interval sets to be created and transformed outside time, group theory enabled Xenakis to generate successions of musical elements "inside time." For example, if one is working with a pitch sieve, group theory procedures might provide the succession of notes drawn from the sieve for a musical passage. But, Xenakis took a more generalized analytical approach in his theoretical thought. Building from his earlier considerations of sonic entities as fundamental building blocks for music—entities defined by parameters such as pitch, loudness, duration, and timbre—he sought in his group theory technique to link successions of these parametrical elements. The relationships between the limited number of elements in the groups ought to be perceived by the listener. He achieved this by creating sets of values (vectors) for each parameter (sieve techniques could be used here, but for a parameter such as amplitude values/dynamics, the subtleties of differing intervallic values would carry little meaning with regard to our perceptual capacity to distinguish them). These parameter value sets were linked through matrices, and a succession of matrix vertices (multi-vector data points) were selected by means of a constrained set of transformations to lead from one to the next.[17] In the case of *Nomos alpha*, Xenakis used the rotational possibilities of a tetrahedron within a cube to set the limits on the transformations.

Outside and Inside

What Xenakis sought was a means of unifying his "outside time" and "inside time" elements while also allowing for material and structural richness. The first

---

[15] Xenakis 1992, 218–36.
[16] Iannis Xenakis, *Arts/Sciences, Alliages* (Tournai: Casterman, 1979); published in English as *Arts/Sciences, Alloys: The Thesis Defense of Iannis Xenakis*, translated by Sharon Kanach (Stuyvesant, NY: Pendragon, 1985).
[17] Xenakis 1992, 210–17, 218–36.

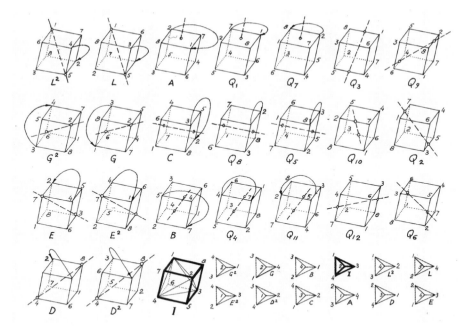

Figure 2.1 Group theory constraints based on rotations of a tetrahedron within a cube

Source: Xenakis 1992, 220.

composition manifesting group theory techniques was *Akrata* (1965) for 16 wind instruments. Xenakis does not discuss it in *Formalized Music*, but he mentions "theory of groups" in reference to *Akrata* in an interview with Mario Bois published around that time.[18] More recently, researcher Stefan Schaub has uncovered sketches in the Xenakis Archives that indicate a much more extensive engagement with this new approach than had been previously thought.[19]

As mentioned earlier, it was *Nomos alpha* (1966) where Xenakis applied his new theories and related compositional techniques most rigorously, and where he thoroughly documented his work. He even annotated his group theory successions onto the score, to make fuller analyses possible.

---

[18] Mario Bois, *Iannis Xenakis, the Man and His Music: A Conversation with the Composer and a Description of His Work* (Paris: Boosey & Hawkes, 1966).

[19] Stefan Schaub, "*Akrata* for 16 winds by Iannis Xenakis: Analyses," in *International Symposium Iannis Xenakis, Athens, May 2005, Definitive Proceedings*, Makis Solomos, Anastasia Georgaki, and Giorgos Zervos, editors (2006 http://cicm.mshparisnord.org/ColloqueXenakis/papers/Schaub.pdf).

Example 2.1 Annotated score excerpt from *Nomos alpha*
Source: Xenakis 1992, 235.

Several researchers have taken on the challenge of analyzing Xenakis's application of his theories in this work, and have even discovered errors and inconsistencies.[20] For Xenakis, however, the algorithms and theories are there to serve the music, in conjunction with the composer's intuitive judgment and creative license:

> I became convinced—and I remain so even today—that one can achieve universality, not through religion, not through emotions or tradition, but through the sciences. Through a scientific way of thinking. But even with that, one can get nowhere without general ideas, points of departure. Scientific thought is only a means through which to realize my ideas, which are not of scientific origin. These ideas are born of intuition, some kind of vision.[21]

---

[20] See Thomas DeLio, "The dialectics of structure and materials: Iannis Xenakis' *Nomos Alpha*," *Journal of Music Theory* 24 (1), 1980. 63–96; Jan Vriend, "'Nomos Alpha' for violoncello solo (Xenakis 1966): Analysis and comments," *Interface* 10, 1981, 15–82.
[21] Varga 1996, 47.

In *Formalized Music*, Xenakis also briefly discusses group theory techniques as applied in his orchestral composition *Nomos gamma* (1968), written just prior to *Kraanerg*. *Nomos gamma* is in fact the last composition Xenakis mentions in his book. His theoretical interests were drawn to another area, that of digital synthesis using stochastic methods. But, it was some years before this research produced musical results (the first being *Polytope de Cluny*, from 1972).

The USA and Beyond

In 1967, Xenakis took up a professorship at Indiana University (IU). His primary research agenda at Bloomington was to develop his computer music interests, in particular his theories regarding stochastic digital synthesis. To accomplish this, he not only had to create the software; he also had to acquire or build a digital-to-analog converter to turn the output of his programs into sound. In the earlier algorithmic work, culminating in his *ST* pieces from 1962, he had transcribed the computer output by hand into musical notation for instruments. The research he undertook at IU during 1967–72 took that work further, bypassing the transcription process to produce computer-generated sound directly. As noted earlier, software-generated sound synthesis had already been developed, most notably by Max Mathews at Bell Labs beginning in 1957; but Xenakis was proposing a completely different model for generating sound using stochastic functions, and such work had certainly never been done before.[22]

While Xenakis was carrying on this research in Bloomington and teaching related courses, he was increasingly busy not only as a composer but also as an invited lecturer. During his sojourn in the USA he visited dozens of universities, giving lectures and presenting concerts, most often of his electroacoustic music. As noted in Chapter 1, his first visit to North America was in 1963, when Aaron Copland invited him to teach composition at the Tanglewood Music Center in Massachusetts. There, he met composer-conductor Lukas Foss, among others. Foss later conducted and recorded works of Xenakis, including *Kraanerg*.

Prior to taking up the teaching post in Bloomington, Xenakis had returned to the USA in the summer of 1966 for the premiere production of the Greek tragedy *Oresteïa* by Aeschylus, directed by Alexis Solomos. As discussed in Chapter 1, writing music for stage was not a major focus for Xenakis, but he was nonetheless enticed into the theater for projects involving the ancient Greek plays he was so devoted to. While the *Oresteïa* drama, presented as part of a festival of Greek plays held in a football stadium in Ypsilanti, Michigan, was presented in English, Xenakis set the chorus parts in Greek, as he was very interested in the classic origins of

---

[22] Xenakis carried on his work in stochastic digital synthesis at EMAMu/CEMAMu in Paris, and the securing of funding there was an important factor in his decision to resign his post at Indiana University.

the language. He came back to the ancient language in later works, particularly his choral compositions *À Colone* (1977) and *À Hélène* (1977).

Dance

With his experience in the theater, and perhaps also with his work in film, Xenakis started to become known in the dance world, and this reputation developed strongly during his time in the USA. *Kraanerg* was his first composition written for dance, but choreographers were already taking up existing works and putting them on stage. The first, and most significant, of these choreographers was George Balanchine. He got his start with Sergei Diaghilev and Les Ballets Russes, the company directed by Diaghilev that launched Igor Stravinsky's career with *The Firebird*, *Petrouchka*, and *The Rite of Spring*. Balanchine carried on the relationship with Stravinsky, creating numerous works with his own company, the New York City Ballet.[23] In January 1968, Balanchine unveiled a new work in two parts, set to Xenakis's early orchestral scores, *Metastaseis* and *Pithoprakta*. The choreography featured two of his star dancers, Suzanne Farrell and Arthur Mitchell. This new dance attracted the attention of the press and the dance public in New York, and it was reprised the following season. Critic Winthrop Sargeant of *The New Yorker* discussed it:

> The music for *Metastaseis & Pithoprakta* is by the Greek composer Iannis Xenakis, an avant-garde hero of the moment, who writes atonally with more than average imagination ... The most absorbing thing about these two ballets ... is the degree to which such a musical substructure can be humanized by means of the dance.[24]

Balanchine seems to have been quite taken with Xenakis. The Xenakis Archives includes documentation of plans for the composer to design a set for the *Metastaseis and Pithoprakta* production in 1969 (which does not seem to have been realized), and the aging choreographer worked on a new choreography using *Bohor* (the eight-channel electroacoustic work from 1962) in 1971, which he unfortunately never mounted. In addition, Balanchine commissioned a new orchestral score from Xenakis. *Antikhthon*, 23 minutes in duration, was completed in 1971, but the choreographer abandoned the project. According to Xenakis (personal communication), the dance was to feature Balanchine's favoured young female principal, Suzanne Farrell, but her acrimonious departure from the New York City Ballet in 1969 caused Balanchine to drop it. The piece has lived on as an

---

[23] The powerful, "primitivist" rhythmic textures often found in Xenakis's music have sometimes been compared to Stravinsky. See Jonathan Cross, *The Stravinsky Legacy* (Cambridge: Cambridge University Press, 2005).

[24] Winthrop Sargeant, "Musical Events," *The New Yorker* (15 February 1969), 96–7.

orchestral composition, but was never choreographed, even after Farrell returned to Balanchine's company in 1975.[25]

Paul Taylor, who worked with both Martha Graham and George Balanchine, created a choreography to Xenakis's chamber work *Atrées* (1963) for his own Paul Taylor Dance Company. *Private Domain* (significantly, this is also the title Taylor later chose for his autobiography) was introduced to New York audiences in May 1969, and was performed elsewhere, including London and Paris. That same spring, in April, preeminent French choreographer Maurice Béjart presented a solo dancer performing to *Nomos alpha* for solo cello, with the cellist performing onstage as well. This took place at the Royan Festival on the Atlantic coast in France, during the same festival as the premiere of *Nomos gamma* (1968), one of Xenakis's large orchestral works where the entire orchestra is distributed amongst the audience to produce a vividly spatial listening experience. In London in May 1969, Norman Morrice created *Them and Us* with the Ballet Rambert to *Eonta* (1963), Xenakis's score for piano and brass.

Architecture and Polytopes

In addition to his increasing activity and visibility as an innovative composer and lecturer in North America (and elsewhere) from the time of his visit to Tanglewood in 1963, Xenakis did not give up on his architectural aspirations. In his 12 years working for Le Corbusier, he had gained a great deal of experience and confidence, although he lacked professional accreditation. As discussed in Chapter 1, he was the project manager acting for Le Corbusier on the Philips Pavilion project for the 1958 World Fair in Brussels, and was granted co-authorship of the building by Le Corbusier to acknowledge the importance of his role in overseeing its design and construction (although obtaining recognition for his work was quite a struggle).[26] Author Sharon Kanach documents numerous architectural projects Xenakis proposed or worked on during his post-Le Corbusier years.[27] He also wrote on the subject, the most significant, and provocative, article being "Cosmic City," from 1964, in which he proposes vertical buildings stretching kilometers into the sky, as a means to address the problems of exponential population growth. This theme of global population would return in his thinking around *Kraanerg*.

---

[25] *Antikhthon* has twice been recorded: Orchestre Philharmonique du Luxembourg, Arturo Tamayo, conductor, Timpani 1C1062, 2001; New Philharmonia Orchestra, Elgar Howarth, conductor, Explore EXP 0017, 2006, originally released on LP in 1976.

[26] Matossian 1986, 129–32.

[27] Sharon Kanach, *Music and Architecture by Iannis Xenakis* (Hillsdale, NY: Pendragon, 2008).

Figure 2.2   *Polytope de Montréal* installation, French Pavilion, 1967

In 1966, Xenakis was invited to create an installation in the French Pavilion for the 1967 World Expo in Montreal. While he may have wanted to design the building himself, architect Jean Faugeron was chosen for the commission. Faugeron designed a huge atrium for the pavilion, accessible on all five levels of the building, fronted by windows overlooking the exposition site and the St. Lawrence River. Xenakis conceived of an installation that would combine sculpture with lighting and music. Dozens of steel cables were stretched from ceiling to floor of the atrium, creating kinetic designs that would be different from every angle and height.

Hundreds of flashbulbs were attached to the cables, and control technology was developed to enable individual control of the lights so they could be switched on and off 25 times a second, a rate that can emulate continuous motion. At that rate, dynamic patterns and progressions could be created. To go with the 6-minute light show, Xenakis created a musical score originally conceived for

Figure 2.3   *Le Diatope*, designed by Iannis Xenakis, 1978

four identical ensembles. The published score for *Polytope de Montréal* indicates that the ensembles should be placed in the four cardinal directions, with the audience placed in the middle. In this way, there would be a sensation of sound movement, as musical events are passed from one ensemble to the next (as a form of spatialized imitation). Such a presentation at the pavilion was not at all practical, though; the musicians would not have been able to perform many times daily for several months. In addition, the visitors would primarily have been viewing/listening from the perimeter of the atrium on several levels, so would not have perceived the spatialization of the sound directly. Documents in the Xenakis Archives indicate that live performance of the music was not seriously considered. Instead, Xenakis installed four loudspeakers on each level pointing out toward the balconies (20 loudspeakers in total). The score was recorded in Paris onto a four-channel tape, and this tape was diffused in the pavilion, each track being routed to its own speaker (on each level). The music was designed to run in tandem with the light show, although they were conceived independently, coinciding only in terms of timing.

By 1967, Xenakis had become very interested in the spatialization of sound. As noted in Chapter 1, his first experience came in 1958 with the Philips Pavilion.[28]

---

[28]   It is worth noting that the individualized string glissandi in *Metastaseis* or the stochastic distribution of sound events across the orchestral strings in *Pithoprakta* produce

Xenakis's short electroacoustic composition, *Concret PH*, was presented there as an interlude between presentations of *Poème électronique*, an audiovisual program conceived by Le Corbusier with music by Varèse. Xenakis's 1962 studio composition, *Bohor*, surrounded the audience with eight loudspeakers diffusing material created on four stereo tracks. In 1963, the composer directed the five brass players in his chamber work *Eonta* to move around the stage and direct their horns in specified directions. With his two orchestral compositions, *Terretektorh* (1966) and *Nomos gamma* (1968)—both premiered at the Royan Festival—Xenakis distributed the individual musicians amongst the audience (requiring a non-standard performance space), producing a highly dynamic, spatialized listening experience that would be different for each listener. *Polytope de Montréal*, then, follows along this trajectory of creative research into the possibilities of movement and directionality of sound. *Kraanerg*, too, with its four-channel electroacoustic component together with a live instrumental ensemble, addresses the issue of sonic spatialization in a significant way.

The powerful multimedia experience of *Polytope de Montréal* created quite a sensation in Montreal. It was one of the highlights of Expo 67, and brought Xenakis to the attention of many people, not only in Montreal but also amongst the numerous visitors to Montreal that year from all across North America and beyond. As listed in Chapter 1, Xenakis went on to produce a number of other multimedia "spectacles," the most significant being *Le Diatope* (1978), for the opening of the Centre Pompidou in central Paris, where he was able to design the pavilion itself. This project was the only time Xenakis was able to truly combine his architectural vision with his compositional interests.

---

quite vivid spatialized textures, given the large space on stage that orchestral strings normally occupy. Nonetheless, this aspect of those orchestral textures does not appear to have been foremost in the composer's mind.

Chapter 3
The *Kraanerg* Project

The story of *Kraanerg* is entwined with a number of others: the National Arts Centre in Ottawa; the National Ballet of Canada; the choreographer Roland Petit; the designer Victor Vasarely; the conductor Lukas Foss; the publisher Boosey & Hawkes; ORTF (Radio France) and Studio Acousti in Paris. It was a commission intended to celebrate the opening of a major arts center in a foreign country, Canada. It was, therefore, a highly prestigious and important project not only for an up-and-coming composer but an artist of even the highest stature.

National Arts Centre

The genesis of the *Kraanerg* project goes back some years to the planning for the National Arts Centre in Ottawa launched in 1963. By that time, the Dominion of Canada was heading towards its centennial celebration, 1 July 1967. The country was beginning to think of itself as a mature nation, led at the time by Lester B. Pearson (1897–1972), a diplomat and statesman who had an active role in the United Nations and NATO before returning to Ottawa to head the Liberal Party of Canada. He was awarded the Nobel Peace Prize in 1957. Ottawa, as the capital city of Canada, suffered from something of an inferiority complex, given that the cultural and economic bases in Canada centered on Montreal and Toronto. With the determination to carve out an identity as the center of state, the National Capital Commission (NCC), formed in 1959, had embarked on long-term plans to raise the city's stature in the country and the world. One of the NCC's most important mandates was the planning of monument and museum sites. Over the years (and still ongoing), a number of such buildings were revitalized or newly designed, including the construction of major sites such as the Canadian Museum of Civilization (architect Douglas Cardinal), renamed the Canadian Museum of History in 2013, and the National Gallery of Canada (architect Moshe Safdie). All of these cultural institutions were intended to cluster about the historic Parliament buildings, with the 92-meter Peace Tower providing a focal point on a bluff overlooking the Ottawa River. In 1963, the National Capital Arts Alliance was founded with the aim of persuading the government to build an arts center that would primarily be devoted to the performing arts. The hope was that the new center would be ready for the centennial celebrations in 1967. A commitment of funding was obtained, and an architect retained.

Fred Lebensold (1917–85), of ARCOP Associates of Montreal, had by that time established a strong reputation as an architect of theaters and performance venues. After studies in Poland, his birthplace, and London, England, he settled in Montreal, establishing an architectural practice and teaching at McGill University. Along with the Queen Elizabeth Theatre in Vancouver and the Fathers of Confederation Memorial Building in Charlottetown, Prince Edward Island, his major achievement was Place des Arts in Montreal, home to the Orchestre Symphonique de Montréal, l'Opéra de Montréal, and Les Grands Ballets Canadiens. Place des Arts was inaugurated in 1963, and Lebensold was soon after engaged to design the new center in Ottawa. The National Arts Centre was to be a similar cultural complex, with three halls/theaters of different sizes (a fourth was added later), rehearsal spaces, restaurants, parking, and ample foyer space for the display of visual art and sculpture. The design was based around a triple hexagon shape, constructed of pebbled concrete. It was created in what is called the Brutalist style, a British term to describe buildings designed from basic geometric shapes constructed from exposed concrete. This style was influenced to a large extent by the post-World War II architectural innovations of Le Corbusier (one of Xenakis's mentors). The modernist plan was controversial, but the boldness of the design ultimately won over a majority of the stakeholders and art-going public.

The scope of the building project and the difficulties in construction (the location on the Rideau Canal, sitting on the exposed granite bedrock of the Canadian Shield,

Figure 3.1   National Arts Centre, Ottawa (photographer unknown, NAC Archives)

certainly slowed progress) meant that the deadline of 1967 passed and the costs quickly mounted. The final expenditure for the building, some $46 million, ended up being about five times more than the original estimate/financial commitment (this sum in current terms would be well over $250 million).

The National Arts Centre Act was proclaimed by the federal government in 1966, with a mandate "to operate and maintain the Centre, to develop the performing arts in the National Capital region, and to assist … in the development of the performing arts elsewhere in Canada." G. Hamilton Southam, a principal instigator of the original Arts Alliance, became the first Director of the NAC. The following year, Southam brought in David Haber (1927–2008) as Director of Programming, and together they began planning not only for the gala festivities, but also for the continuing activities of the NAC. Haber came to Ottawa from Montreal, where he had organized the World Festival of the Performing Arts for Expo 67. He had also been associated with the National Ballet during its earliest, formative years.

National Ballet of Canada

The National Ballet of Canada, based in Toronto, was established in 1951, its first Artistic Director being Celia Franca (1921–2007), who remained at the helm until 1975. Prior to coming to Canada, she had been building a career as a dancer and choreographer in her native London, primarily associated with the Metropolitan Ballet and Sadler's Wells, which became The Royal Ballet in 1946, resident in the newly opened Covent Garden Royal Opera House. Her style was influenced by British choreographer Frederick Ashton (1904–88), founding choreographer of The Royal Ballet. His greatest protégée was Margot Fonteyn (1919–91), who enjoyed a long and starred career, notably in partnership with Rudolf Nureyev (1938–93), who began dancing with her in 1961 after defecting from the Kirov Ballet.

In Toronto, a group of dance enthusiasts had been working to set up a new company, and in order to anchor it they enticed Franca to move to Canada to spearhead the project. With enormous energy and discipline, she built the Toronto company up to international level; and, with Betty Oliphant, created a training school in 1959 that accepted student dancers from across the country. Frank Augustyn and Karen Kain (current Artistic Director of the National Ballet) were two early graduates of the school who went on to careers as principal dancers of the company and beyond. The National Ballet has a reputation as a "classical" company, performing works from the repertoire, including an annual winter holiday run of Tchaikovsky's *The Nutcracker*.

In Ottawa, NAC Director Southam knew Franca, as did Haber, and they also knew that the National Ballet toured throughout Canada as well as internationally. Southam first contacted her in 1966 to discuss in general terms having the company perform at the NAC once it was in operation. By August 1967, with Haber onboard at the NAC, Southam was firming up plans to have the National Ballet be part of the gala opening. The NAC did not yet have any resident performing companies based in Ottawa, so it was clear that imported talent would be necessary. The NAC Orchestra was established later in 1969, and has been resident there ever since, with Jean-Marie Beaudet as first Music Director.

The National Ballet was a large company, with its own orchestra, that worked with star dancers and guest choreographers. Rudolf Nureyev first danced with the National Ballet in 1965, and later took the company with him to perform at the Lincoln Center in New York in 1972. By 1969, the company's highly respected reputation ensured that its presence in Ottawa for the gala opening of the NAC would attract national and international attention and prestige to the event.

As planning for the gala opening progressed, Southam and Haber in Ottawa made it clear that the NAC wanted Franca to bring in a star, and Nureyev was the star of preference, possibly together with Fonteyn.[1] During this period their partnership was setting the dance world on fire. As principal dancers of The Royal Ballet in London, the famed duo would not have easily been free to come to Canada, especially to dance in a new work they did not already know. Perhaps, though, it could have been possible if they were coming to Canada to work with a choreographer they did already know.

Roland Petit

By 1968, when he was brought onboard for the NAC gala, Roland Petit (1924–2011) had established a solid international reputation as an eclectic, forward-looking French choreographer.

At the young age of 21, after training at the Paris Opera Ballet (from age nine) and beginning his career there (interrupted by the war and Nazi occupation of Paris), he founded his first ballet company, the Ballets des Champs-Élysées. Subsequently, he created Les Ballets de Paris in 1948, which carried on, intermittently, until his appointment as Director of the Paris Opera Ballet in 1970. This prestigious position was brief, and he spent most of the rest of his career at the helm of the Ballet National de Marseilles. His first major success as a choreographer was an erotic, dramatic setting of *Carmen* (premiered in London in 1949) that over the years has been programmed by many dance companies around the world. Another early success was *Les Demoiselles de la Nuit* (1948), in which Margot Fonteyn took on the sensuous role of Agathe the cat-woman. *Le Jeune Homme et la Mort*, from 1946, was turned into a film in 1966 by the choreographer, featuring the highly photogenic Nureyev.

Petit early on showed a predilection for working with contemporary composers, collaborating with many of the important French musicians of the day, including: Georges Auric, Henri Dutilleux, Jean Françaix, Maurice Jarre, Marcel Landowski, Olivier Messiaen, and Darius Milhaud. Composer-conductor Marius Constant began

---

[1] Many of the details around this gala event that came to include *Kraanerg* have been found in letters and notes preserved in the archives of the National Ballet of Canada.

Figure 3.2   Roland Petit, choreographer (photograph, National Ballet of Canada)

working with Petit in 1956 as Music Director of Les Ballets de Paris, creating scores for several works. Petit also staged several "revues" to popular music by George Gershwin, Cole Porter, Pink Floyd, and others. These shows inevitably featured his long-time romantic partner and muse, Zizi Jeanmaire. In the 1950s the pair were enticed to visit Hollywood, choreographing (Roland) and dancing (Zizi) for a number of films, including: *Hans Christian Andersen* with Danny Kaye (1952), *Daddy Long Legs* with Fred Astaire and Leslie Caron (1954), and *Anything Goes* with Bing Crosby (1955). His experience in Hollywood would later help Petit make the film with Nureyev for French television (ORTF), which he directed himself.

In 1967, following on from filming *Le Jeune Homme et la Mort* in 1966, Petit worked with the Royal Ballet in London to create a new work, *Paradise Lost*, featuring Nureyev and Fontaine. The music was composed by Marius Constant. The following year, Petit created another ballet for Nureyev with Italian ballerina Luciana Savignano, *Ecstasy* (to music by Alexander Scriabin), for La Scala in Milan.

At the time when the National Ballet of Canada was looking for a prestigious choreographer for its NAC gala show, Roland Petit's name would have been very much in the air, for his work in films, his successful shows in Paris, his international touring, and especially for his work with Nureyev. According to critic Clement Crisp, Petit was known for "visual sophistication," "dramatic clarity," and creating "roles that encourage a dancer to shine."[2] It was also possible, however, to see that "his identification with [the] young, sexy and theatrical tended to brand Petit as a showman rather than as a major ballet choreographer."[3] This showmanship aspect of his reputation was underscored by his ownership and operation of the Casino de Paris in 1970–75.

Regardless of where one stood regarding Petit's reputation, he was very much present in the upper echelons of the international dance world when Celia Franca and National Ballet General Manager Wallace Russell were looking for a choreographer for the NAC gala. The first correspondence with Petit found in the National Ballet archive dates from March 1968. A contract was signed in September. By late March, the choreographer reported that Nureyev would not be available, and mention is made of soloist Edward Villella, then a principal dancer with the New York City Ballet (he would not have danced in Balanchine's *Metastaseis & Pithoprakta*, as it starred Farrell and Mitchell, but he would likely have known of it). At the same time, in March 1968, the correspondence mentions Marius Constant as composer for the NAC gala project.

The archive documents an interesting exchange of creative ideas as the project developed over the spring and summer of 1968. Jean-Paul Riopelle (1923–2002), one of Canada's foremost abstract expressionist artists, was raised by Franca and Russell as a possible designer for the show (he was living in France at that time, but may not have been known to Petit). A possible subject for the ballet was mentioned by Petit, based on the life of Vladimir Mayakowsky, a provocative Russian poet and playwright known as a Futurist, who shot himself in 1930. He was part of the Bolshevik Revolution, but was criticized for being too avant-garde. This idea for a

---

[2] Clement Crisp, "Roland Petit," *Financial Times* (27 July 2011).
[3] Ismene Brown, "Roland Petit," *The Arts Desk* (10 July 2011).

scenario was thought (by Franca) to be too controversial for the occasion, especially in light of the political upheavals going on around the globe by the summer of 1968 (although, as we shall see, these upheavals would be addressed by Xenakis in his notes for the piece that was eventually created). Up until July 1968, Petit was mentioning Marius Constant as composer for the project in his letters to Franca and Russell. After all, he had an ongoing relationship with Constant going back to 1956, and they had just been working together on *Paradise Lost* for the Royal Ballet in London.

Bringing in Xenakis

At the same time as he was working as Music Director for Petit's company in Paris, Constant created the Ensemble Ars Nova in 1963, a resident ensemble of Radio France (ORTF) dedicated to performing and broadcasting/recording new music. He conducted numerous works over several years, performing mostly in Paris, but also touring: Ensemble Ars Nova appeared in Montreal to play for one of the earliest concerts of the Société de Musique Contemporaine du Québec (SMCQ) in November 1967.[4] Over the years, several recordings were issued, including two featuring the music of Xenakis: one presenting the concert version of *Oresteïa*; the other presenting *Polytope de Montréal* for four ensembles (this recording by Constant was used for the installation at the French Pavilion in Montreal), *Syrmos* for strings, and the concert suite from *Medea*. Later, *Kraanerg* was also released on LP (to be discussed later), conducted and recorded by Constant and Ensemble Ars Nova, eventually forming part of a five-disc box set issued by Erato.

Constant was busy, clearly, as a composer, conductor, and music director. He turned down the job of creating the music for the gala in Ottawa, and it is quite possible that he recommended Xenakis in his place. It is also possible that Petit would already have known of Xenakis, given the dance performances to his music occurring right around that time in New York, London, and France. In any case, the choreographer mentioned Xenakis in a letter to Franca and Russell in July 1968. By mid-August, Petit had spoken to the composer about the project and had gotten his accord, and Russell followed up by writing to Xenakis soon after. After this initial contact, with nine months to go before the opening, the details began to quickly fall into place.

---

[4] When Constant appeared in Montreal late in 1967, Xenakis's *Polytope de Montréal* had just finished its run of several months at the World Expo there. The SMCQ performed his *Eonta* in March 1969.

Kraanerg Comes Together

According to Petit, "We started without a story line. I made the ballet as a sculptor makes a sculpture."[5] This was a wise choice on his part, to leave Xenakis free to create the music according to his own dictates. The choreographer was confident he could create a ballet to whatever music Xenakis came up with. It would nonetheless be a challenge, as this was to be a full-length work, 75 minutes in duration. Petit was scheduled to come to Canada in April 1969, to work with the company and develop the work. The music had to be completed and recorded by then, so they could rehearse to it. Petit ended up bringing in three guest soloists: Edward Villella, from the New York City Ballet; Georges Piletta, from the Paris Opera Ballet; and Lynn Seymour (a Canadian dancer), from the Berlin Opera Ballet.

It was Xenakis who thought to suggest op-art innovator Victor Vasarely as designer for the ballet. He had come into contact with the artist in 1960, when he did the soundtrack to a short film on a Vasarely exhibition in Paris. Op-art is a style of visual design based on optical illusion. In Vasarely's case, he mainly worked with simple geometric forms like squares and circles, shading them and carefully combining colours to create an impression of three-dimensionality. With Petit in agreement, the National Ballet was able to bring Vasarely (and his son Yvaral, also an artist) onboard. Xenakis's contract gave him the power to choose a conductor. While the National Ballet had a Musical Director, George Crum (who would be called on to conduct subsequent performances in Toronto and on tour), the avant-garde nature of the music called for a specialist. Xenakis at first suggested Seiji Ozawa, whom he had met in 1961 on his first trip to Tokyo. Ozawa had already conducted music by Xenakis, and was at that time resident nearby, as Music Director of the Toronto Symphony Orchestra (1965–69). When it turned out that Ozawa would be on tour and unavailable for the premiere in Ottawa, Xenakis proposed Lukas Foss, then based in Buffalo, New York, also nearby. Foss was a composer and conductor, and had recently performed orchestral works of Xenakis, in Paris and with the Buffalo Philharmonic Orchestra.

With the designer, conductor, and dance soloists in place for the NAC gala, there remained some important details regarding the music to be worked out. A crucial one concerned the instrumentation. The National Ballet, in its agreement with Boosey & Hawkes, Xenakis's publisher, had agreed to 50 performances over two years, in exchange for exclusive rights to the music. The company intended to tour the work, to showcase it internationally. A standard chamber orchestra was normally used, to cover all the repertoire the company might present. Xenakis proposed some alterations to the instrumentation, summarized as follows in Table 3.1.

---

[5] Roland Petit, "Press release" (Ottawa: National Arts Centre, May 1969).

Table 3.1   Comparison of Xenakis's *Kraanerg* instrumentation with the standard National Ballet of Canada orchestra

National Ballet touring orchestra	*Kraanerg* instrumentation
Flute (doubling piccolo)	Piccolo
Oboe	Oboe
Clarinet I	E♭ clarinet
Clarinet II (doubling bass)	Bass clarinet (doubling contrabass)
Bassoon	Contrabass bassoon
Trumpet I	Trumpet I
Trumpet II	Trumpet II
Horn I	Horn I
Horn II	Horn II
Trombone	Trombone I
	Trombone II
Piano	
Percussion	
Violin I (4)	Violin I (3)
Violin II (2)	Violin II (3)
Viola (2)	
Cello (2)	Cello (3)
Double bass	Double bass (3)
23	23 (8 non-overlapping)

As this chart shows, Xenakis required the contrabass clarinet and contrabassoon, instruments that are not standard doublings for clarinet and bassoon players. He also needed an extra trombone, and an additional cello and two double basses. Presumably, the instruments he did not require would have been needed for other repertoire, so there would be no savings by his leaving out instruments such as piano and percussion. His instrumentation required eight extra players, in fact, even though the number of musicians needed was the same. Wallace Russell was also concerned with playability, as the company would normally underwrite minimal rehearsal time with the orchestra, as most of the rehearsal time with the dancers is done with a rehearsal pianist, or, in this case, a recording. Xenakis, however, had a reputation for writing scores that pushed the boundaries of ordinary instrumental techniques, and this piece was to be no exception. The composer was not all that concerned with the practical issues of performability based on minimal rehearsal. His reputation had been made on introducing novel sonorities, textures, and intensity of expression in his music, not on composing accessible, easy-to-play scores. As it turned out, the National Ballet of Canada would end up performing *Kraanerg* a total of 19 times through 1972, nowhere near the 50 performances they agreed to pay royalties on to Boosey & Hawkes.

Electronics and Recording

Another issue to be tackled concerned the technical aspects of the electroacoustic element of the music. In order to showcase the state-of-the-art sound system installed at the NAC, Xenakis was asked to add an electronic part to his score. In addition to loudspeakers in the side walls of the auditorium, there were speakers in the wall below the balcony, in the ceiling, in a cluster above the proscenium, and onstage (portable speakers that could be placed where necessary). There were two four-track reel-to-reel tape recorders for playback, so sound spatialization was possible. In addition to his score for 23 instruments, Xenakis chose to create a four-channel electroacoustic component that would be played back from tape and surround the audience. This tape part would be just as significant as the scored part, and even though Xenakis ended up composing the music to run continuously for the entire duration, he did foresee the eventual need for a break so that the sound engineer could switch from one tape machine to the other (recorders could handle reels of 40 minutes duration maximum). He mentioned this requirement in correspondence with the National Ballet, but he did not compose the music with such a break built into the conception of the work's formal design. While the inclusion of the electroacoustic element served the purposes of the NAC well, by highlighting the technological innovations of its brand-new sound system, it would be one more barrier to touring for the National Ballet, as other venues may well not have had the requisite sound system installed, necessitating additional logistical burden and expense.

As we have seen, Xenakis himself already had quite a bit of experience both in the electronic music studio and in working with spatialized sound, in recorded material as well as live performance. His eight-channel electroacoustic work, *Bohor*, had the loudspeakers surrounding the audience to provide an intensely immersive experience. His *Polytope de Montréal* utilized a four-track recording of an instrumental score that was projected from 20 loudspeakers incorporated into his multimedia installation. And, just before he embarked on this new project for Ottawa, Xenakis was finishing up the score for *Nomos gamma*, a composition for spatialized orchestra where the individual instruments are scattered amongst the audience, all surrounded by eight percussionists. For *Kraanerg*, Xenakis was able to explore the interplay between spatialized sound coming from the loudspeakers and live sound coming from the orchestra pit. This was his first experience working with live musicians and recorded sound; his only other mixed composition is *Pour la Paix*, for voices and electronic sound, produced in 1982.

The main obstacle Xenakis faced in completing the electroacoustic part of *Kraanerg* was his lack of access to a studio. His affiliation with GRM in Paris ended in 1962, and Indiana University, where he was teaching by this time, did not have an appropriate facility for him to work in. At that time, most studio-based compositional work was carried out at institutional facilities, either state-funded studios such as GRM and elsewhere in Europe (usually affiliated with national broadcasting organizations) or university-based studios. With neither option open to him, Xenakis booked time at a private studio in Paris to get the work done. Studio Acousti did not have the specialized, custom-built equipment that Xenakis had used at GRM (such as the Phonogène, a variable-speed tape recorder controllable from an electronic keyboard), but it had the ability to record instruments and do basic processing and mixing.

Perhaps as a result of these limitations, Xenakis chose to restrict the sonic possibilities for *Kraanerg* to recording the same instruments he was using for the live part of the score, treating the winds and strings as separate entities in the studio. The main alterations he subjected these ensemble recordings to were: tape speed change, where the pitch and duration of the recording could be altered; filtering, where he could affect the frequency profile of the sounds; distortion, where the amplitude profile could be altered to change the tone quality; and reverberation, where aspects of distance and location could be manipulated. The other main effort in the studio concerned mixing the winds and strings together and then spatializing them onto four channels.

One of the sound engineers at Studio Acousti at the time, Bruno Menny, was also an electroacoustic composer, whose album of experimental studio work, *Cosmographie*, was released in 1972. In 1968, Guy Chalon and Yuri Korolkoff, also of Studio Acousti, recorded sounds of the student demonstrations in the streets of Paris in May of that year. The studio released a disc of these documentary sounds, and it is possible that Xenakis heard this recording. Even though he was working in Bloomington at that time, Matossian reports that he was very much in touch with the protests in Paris, following the news reports with great interest.[6] Xenakis continued to collaborate with Studio Acousti on electroacoustic projects until his own facility, CEMAMu, was self-sufficient. Today, the studio continues to function in the sixth *arrondissement*, in the heart of Paris.

Xenakis faced another constraint: the need to have the entire piece recorded for rehearsal use. This meant getting the musicians together to record the score, then mixing this with a stereo version of the studio-produced four-track tape part. With the support of Constant and Ensemble Ars Nova and their association with Radio France, he was able to use the facilities there, including the GRM studio, to get this recording and mixing done. Given that the National Ballet needed the recording by April 1969 at the latest in order to begin work on the piece, Xenakis also tried to find a record label interested in issuing the studio recording on LP, ideally in time for the premiere. The most likely candidate was Erato, a French label known for early music but also for releasing recordings of new music. While it did not happen by June, Erato did issue the recording of *Kraanerg* later that year, not on its own but, as mentioned earlier, bundled with other recordings of Xenakis's orchestral, ensemble, and electroacoustic music in a five-disc box set. This recording gives credit to Guy Laporte as recording engineer and Bernard Laroux as mixing engineer. Both jobs would have been extremely demanding, particularly as the music runs for

---

[6] Matossian 1986, 195.

75 minutes without a break (*Kraanerg* was broken into four parts for this release, taking up both sides of two LPs).

Programme and Staging

Early on in the compositional process, Xenakis came up with the title, *Kraanerg*. This is a composite word made up of two Greek terms: "kraan," meaning to accomplish, to perfect; and "erg," meaning energy. In the press release put out by the NAC prior to the gala premiere, Xenakis explains that "the ballet has no symbolism but is a dialogue on the ideological disorders that will face the world when mushrooming birthrates mean 70 or 80 per cent of the population is younger than 30."[7] The composer, a former Greek Resistance fighter, distanced himself from current affairs by looking to global processes unfolding over decades or longer. He did not distance himself entirely, however, as by the summer of 1968 the youth of many parts of the world were protesting in the streets, advocating various concerns from civil rights and political freedoms to accessible education to the Vietnam War, and more. While Xenakis was careful to not tie his work to then-current struggles, perhaps partly to avoid political controversy and partly to avoid any risk of datedness, he nonetheless found a way to include the upheavals going on around him within his more general vision. While Petit avoided any controversy in his introductory notes for the program booklet, concentrating mainly on the dance and the décor, conductor Lukas Foss had no misgivings about noting the wider implications of the work: "People will ask 'Is it art?' Art is that thing that can afford to be violent without harming."[8]

While the music for *Kraanerg* will be examined in detail in the next chapter, some attention can be paid to the stage design and choreography here. With no narrative or script, just non-referential music, both Vasarely and Petit had a great deal of freedom to carry out their own creative work. While these two did communicate with each other and with Xenakis as they went along, contact was minimal, each working quite independently. Petit did not really start working on his choreography until he arrived in Canada in April 1969. By that time, Xenakis's work was done, and Vasarely was already well along in his designs. He collaborated with his son, Yvaral, who made the trip to Canada to oversee the installation of the designs. The artist chose to work with black and white (not unusual for him), with the dancers also dressed in either black or white leotards. The backdrop was black with white vertical ribbons hung in front. The usual illusion of movement that is conveyed by such stripes fixed onto a canvas was made even more manifest by the ability of the white ribbons to move slightly, creating kinetic patterns of shadow and light. Onto this were juxtaposed outlines of a large circle and a large square. Overhead, a large

---

[7] Iannis Xenakis, "Press release" (Ottawa: National Arts Centre, May 1969).
[8] Lukas Foss, "Press release" (Ottawa: National Arts Centre, May 1969).

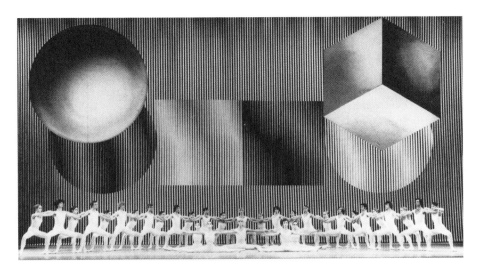

Figure 3.3   One view of stage design by Vasarely for *Kraanerg*

Figure 3.4   Second view of stage design by Vasarely for *Kraanerg*

cube and sphere were suspended, covered with a white metallic surface that could reflect distorted images of the dancers below, depending on placement and lighting. Petit underscored the symbolic as well as the geometric significance of these basic shapes in his introductory notes for the program booklet: "In ancient times the circle symbolized earthly paradise and the square, celestial paradise. However, in topology, these two symbols have the same significance."[9]

By these simple, but powerful means, Vasarely was able to achieve a great deal of dynamism and energy in his stage design, befitting of the meaning of the work's title. His design worked in conjunction with the lighting, which was overseen by National Ballet General Manager Wallace Russell, who had also been the company's Lighting Designer for many years.

The Choreography

When Petit received the recording of *Kraanerg* from Xenakis in March 1969, he was faced with a monolithic work, running continuously for 75 minutes. There are no movements, although there are clearly delineated blocks of sound, the primary shifts occurring as the music switches between the live ensemble and the studio-produced segments. The music contains silences, but they do not mark sections; they seem to function as almost equal elements of the composition. In addition, there is very little sense of pulse or meter in the music.

Without a story to set, the choreographer adopted a relatively classical approach to creating his work. That is, he developed a series of set pieces featuring soloists and/or ensemble. This would be the same approach a choreographer might take in setting a classical concert work to dance. Given the length, he decided to create an intermission at about the halfway point (something Xenakis had foreseen, as mentioned earlier). A summary of Petit's work is given in Table 3.2, adapted from the printed program, with durations taken from archival documentation.

Clearly, Petit sought to feature the soloists and the company in different combinations. Guest dancer Georges Piletta dominates the first half, with Lynn Seymour not highlighted at all until after the intermission. It is puzzling that the other guest soloist, Edward Villella, is not listed in the details of the movements (although he is noted in the program). Was he filling out the male section of the company? Was he an understudy for Piletta? From existing documentation in the National Ballet archives, the answers to these questions are unclear.

What is also unclear is how Petit made his decisions about where movements would begin, in coordination with the music. At times, he begins a new movement with a new segment of music. At other times, though, a movement coincides with a silence, or with the end of a silence; or, it begins in the middle of a musical segment.

---

[9] Roland Petit, "Synopsis," *Kraanerg* program booklet (Ottawa: National Arts Centre/ National Ballet of Canada, 1969).

Table 3.2 Choreographic movements for *Kraanerg* by Roland Petit

Movements	Dancers (guest soloists in bold, company principals named)	Timings (duration)
Curtain		0:00 (2′48″)
I	**Georges Piletta**	2:48 (6′00″)
II	**Georges Piletta** and Girls	8:48 (2′30″)
III	Karen Bowes, Mary Jago, **Georges Piletta**	11:18 (6′08″)
IV	**Georges Piletta**, Clinton Rothwell and Boys	17:26 (6′12″)
V	Veronica Tennant and Girls	23:38 (3′10″)
VI	Veronica Tennant, David Gordon, Andrew Oxenham	26:48 (5′32″)
VII	Karen Bowes, Mary Jago, **Georges Piletta** and Ensemble	32:20 (5′32″)
Intermission		37:52
Curtain		37:52 (2′18″)
VIII	**Georges Piletta** and Timothy Spain	40:10 (6′36″)
IX	**Lynn Seymour** and Boys	46:46 (4′08″)
X	**Lynn Seymour** and **Georges Piletta**	50:54 (8′15″)
XI	Karen Bowes, Mary Jago, Clinton Rothwell, Veronica Tennant, David Gordon, Andrew Oxenham, Timothy Spain, **Lynn Seymour**, **Georges Piletta** and Ensemble	59:09 (16′02″)
Curtain		75:11

The intermission, while very close to the halfway point, otherwise seems pretty arbitrary, coming in the middle of an ensemble segment, though the break at least occurs where there is a 2-second silence notated in the score. Each movement is relatively brief, ranging from 2 to 6 minutes, with the exception of the final two movements of the second part.

While the two parts of Petit's form are equal in terms of overall duration, the first part is much more elaborate in terms of his deployment of different dancers and combinations of dancers. The durations would likely have been primarily a result of the working out of sequences of dance moves. In the second part, there is more variability in the sequencing of movements. The *pas-de-deux* featuring Piletta and Seymour lasts for 8 minutes, longer than any of the movements in the first part, while the finale, featuring everyone, is just about double the length of the preceding duo. This movement would have been made up of a number of sequences and combinations.[10]

We will return to the critical reception of *Kraanerg* in Chapter 5, including subsequent settings by other choreographers. Suffice it to say at this point that the

---

[10] The archives at the National Ballet of Canada contain no notes from Petit on the choreography, unfortunately.

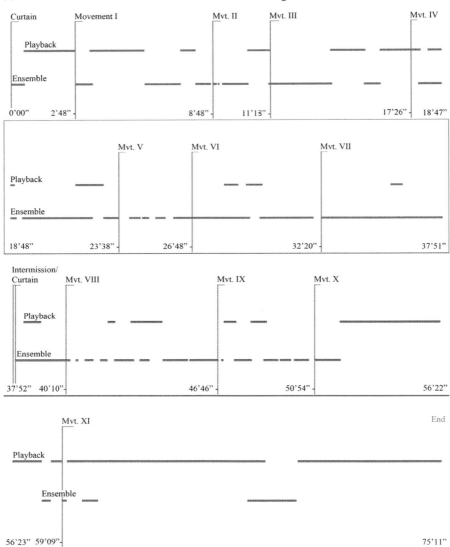

Figure 3.5   Outline of *Kraanerg* showing basic score segments with ballet timings

radical sonorities and relentlessly continuous formal design of the music posed a strong challenge to a choreographer used to working with narratives or set pieces. A more avant-garde figure such as Merce Cunningham may have been better suited to working with such music. Be that as it may, Petit created an admirably workable piece in the two months he had with the National Ballet of Canada. Dignitaries and

The Kraanerg *Project*

Figure 3.6   Soloist Lynn Seymour with Pierre Elliott Trudeau, Prime Minister of Canada

critics from the world over were invited to the gala performance in Ottawa. Pierre Elliott Trudeau, the dashing, charismatic Prime Minister of Canada—elected just the year before (and representing, in a way, the youthful generation Xenakis had in mind while composing his work)—was in attendance, along with Roland Michener, Governor General of Canada, and the cream of the diplomatic circles in Ottawa and the artistic world of Canada and beyond. Along with the premiere of this new work, the gala was a party to celebrate the opening of a major new arts center, an indicator of cultural optimism more than concern over world upheaval.

Chapter 4
Kraanerg Analysis

Preliminary Sketches

Xenakis signed the commission contract with the National Ballet of Canada on 21 September 1968. The Xenakis Archives reveals a sketch dated that same day, in which he pencils in the title, *Kraanerg* (spelled a few different ways). This is quite significant, indicating that the composer had an intuitive idea of the music that likely served to guide him through the compositional process. That same sketch includes listings of different musical parameters, indicating Xenakis was thinking of adopting an approach guided by the group theory techniques he had developed in previous pieces such as *Akrata*, *Nomos alpha*, and *Nomos gamma*. There are six columns in this listing:

1. Instruments: a list that includes instruments (notably percussion) that he didn't end up using. It's likely that the definitive instrumentation agreed upon by both Xenakis and the National Ballet hadn't yet been arrived at.
2. Registers: there are five listed, from extreme high to extreme low. This may have guided the composer's thinking in settling on instruments such as piccolo and E♭ clarinet, and contrabass clarinet and contrabassoon that could cover the extreme ranges for the winds.
3. Playing mode: these include normal held notes, quilisma (a term Xenakis uses to indicate slow, irregular glissandi fluctuating around a given pitch), trill, flutter-tongue (one could presume this to also include string tremolo), and staccato (which would likely also include repeated staccato notes).
4. Dynamics: the mid-range dynamics are crossed out, so only the extremes of loud and soft are listed.
5. Density: this indicates the number of instruments playing at a time, from solo to duo, etc.
6. Sonic entities: in this column Xenakis draws graphic indications for parallel glissandi, crossing glissandi, a cloud of short notes, and a cloud of mixed short and longer notes.

There is another intriguing column in this sketch that is not labeled, containing titles of existing compositions: *Akrata, Polytope de Montréal, Nomos alpha*. *Akrata* has a graphic design beside it indicating repeated staccato notes, while *Polytope* has some wavy lines beside it, likely indicating quilisma (this sonority is a key feature of that work). Xenakis would seem to have had particular textures in mind here, the listing of titles constituting a form of shorthand for his own use. Elsewhere, the sketches also include notes mentioning *Eonta*, *Nomos gamma*, and *Nuits*. There is no mention in this initial sketch of the electroacoustic element.

Other sketches include notes on "sections," with the numbers 15–8–8–11 adding up to 42. It is difficult to say what this numerical breakdown means, but the piece does turn out to be put together from approximately 42 sections, as we shall see (there are some ambiguities in defining sections in the score—our analysis settles on 44). He also jots down the calculation of total duration (75) into number of sections (42) to arrive at an average section duration of 1.78 (or 1′47″). Again, the actual segment durations turn out to be different, mainly because of how they sometimes overlap. Other sketches show timelines for the piece, with layers of markings of different colors (but with no obvious key to the musical or structural layers represented there). These are all tantalizing clues to the compositional process of *Kraanerg* and can provide an analytical point of departure.

There are actually, though, very few sketches for *Kraanerg* in the archives, unfortunately. There are no drafts of the score, no detailed musical annotations, no working out of the formal structure using his group theory approach. There is almost nothing in the archives about how the studio-recorded portions of the piece were created (although there are sketches showing consideration of the four channels of the tape, to be discussed below). If Xenakis had proceeded with his initial thoughts regarding formal organization by means of group theory processes, there should be a great deal of detailed working out of all the particulars, as is found for *Nomos alpha* and to a lesser extent for *Akrata* and *Nomos gamma*. While it is possible that the sketches were lost, close examination of the score confirms that the systematic deployment of the listed parameters in *Kraanerg* is not particularly rigorous. The best estimate of compositional approach is that Xenakis used the group theory approach as a guide to his thinking, but that he worked more intuitively. And actually, for the most part, he worked more intuitively from this point in his career onward, publishing very little theoretical work, producing often fairly minimal sketch materials, and discussing his music mostly in interviews, revealing just occasional glimpses of the inner workings.

The Score

The score of *Kraanerg* is an interesting and informative document in its own right. A copy of the composer's manuscript, the layout of the music, is quite particular. The musical material appears to have been cut out from manuscript paper and affixed to large blank sheets, with the winds and strings laid into the score separately. The timing (in minutes and seconds) is included in order that the conductor and tape machine operator remain synchronized. It helps that the tempo is invariable at two seconds per measure (each measure being $\frac{1}{4}$). There are 20 tape segments, requiring very precise starting and stopping, with the score indicating the exact timing to be followed. Sometimes there are overlaps between ensemble and playback, sometimes one follows directly after the other, sometimes there is measured silence between the segments. Both the conductor and machine operator must work with stopwatches (or similar technology). Where the recorded sounds play on alone, the score is blank except for a horizontal line across the page, timings indicated on the next page where the ensemble enters again.

The recorded segments were created from sessions involving what is most likely the same ensemble as the *Kraanerg* ensemble score (there is no archival confirmation of the instrumentation used, but close listening does not identify any other instruments such as percussion or piano, nor any higher density of instruments such as orchestral string sections). The archive contains recordings from these sessions, in the form of 40-minute tapes of music that continues without break. There are two tapes (making approximately 80 minutes of material in total) for the winds and strings separately. There is no indication that individual instruments were recorded separately and mixed down later. It is most likely that a single recording session of the full ensemble was captured all at once, or perhaps separate sessions for winds and strings. These recordings, available in the Xenakis Archives, were already processed in the studio; there are no other materials of the recording/production process, including score material used for the sessions (aside from the Annexes appended to the end of the score, to be discussed below). These recordings at least confirm that the material the winds and strings performed in the studio was not derived from the score for the live ensemble. However, given that the published score for *Kraanerg* was copied and pasted from another source, one could conjecture that the original material for both ensemble and recorded segments could perhaps be the same. There is no way to confirm this speculation, however, until or unless further materials are discovered. It is worth noting that the total duration of the recorded segments used in the piece totals just under 40 minutes (broken into 20 segments). Given some overlap, the total duration of the ensemble segments is about the same.

In the score, it is clear that, at times, Xenakis cut longer, continuous material into excerpts that he pasted into different, not necessarily successive, segments in the score. One example comes at 12′04″, where the winds join an ongoing segment of strings that begins at 11′12″. The winds drop out by 12′29″, while the strings continue. The winds enter again at 12′48″–13′10″, but this block is different material (this excerpt actually continues at 18′14″–19′16″). The continuation of the material from 12′04″ to 12′30″ picks up again at 13′24″–13′52″. In the score, the way in which the systems are cut clearly indicates these excerpts were originally connected.

The long, continuous string segment finishes at 14′00″, followed by a recorded segment running from 13′56″ to 15′28″. The strings pick up again, clearly continuing where they left off. At 15′44″, the winds enter over the ongoing strings, carrying on from where they left off at 13′54″. Again, the score clearly shows how the source material was cut into excerpts. There are numerous similar instances of material for either winds or strings that are cut from a source score and pasted into different spots in the performance score.

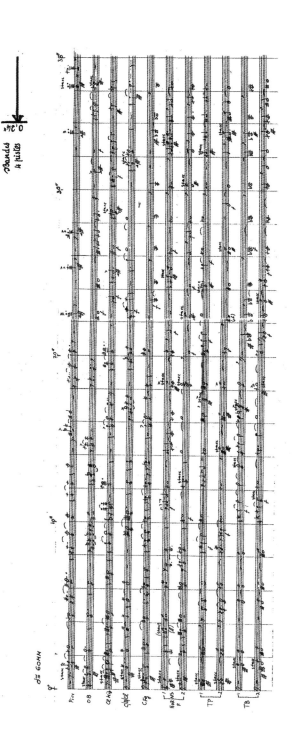

Example 4.1 Page 1 of *Kraanerg* score, showing timing for the electronic part

Example 4.2 Page 4 of *Kraanerg* score

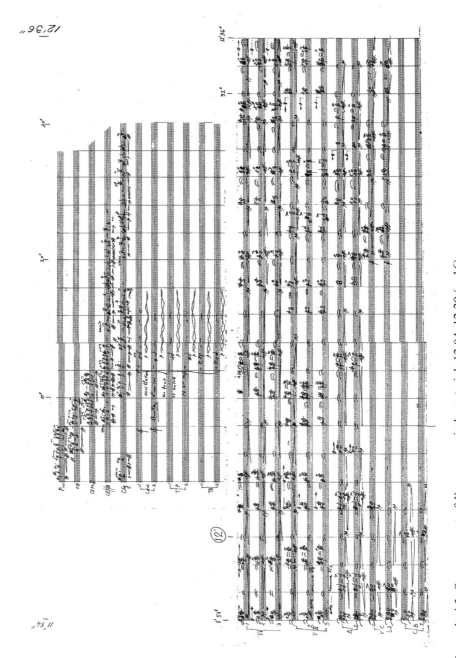

Example 4.3 Score excerpt of *Kraanerg*, winds material: 12:04–12:29 (p. 16)

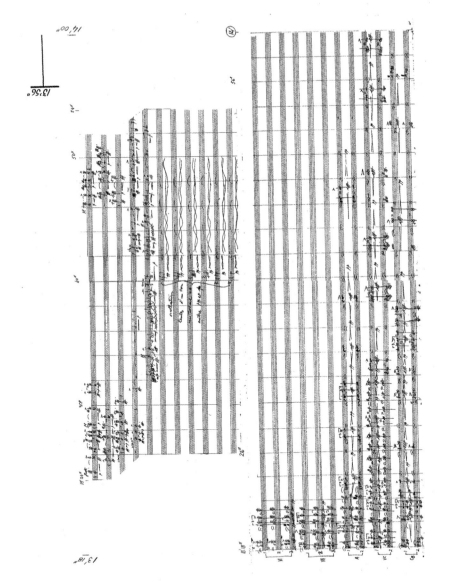

Example 4.4 Score excerpt of *Kraanerg*, continuation of winds material: 13:24–13:52 (p. 18)

It is possible, and even likely, that a similar, nonlinear process of cutting ongoing music into blocks, winds and strings being treated separately, was applied to the studio recordings used for the recorded segments. There are sketches that indicate some kind of plan for the tape, but there are no precise indications of how the segments were put together. When one listens to them in isolation, though, it is very obvious that the material does not have clearly articulated starting and stopping gestures, as if the segments were planned as autonomous entities; instead, they seem to be cut out from ongoing textures, and often the next segment sounds as if it could have continued from the previous one. It is also clear that the segments are pieced together from independent blocks of winds and strings material in a very similar way as the score. It seems that Xenakis mixed the two tapes of winds and strings material to create two layers of each, as there are often two layers of distinctive wind and string textures sounding at the same time. In addition to the processing of the recorded sounds, one of the main distinguishing features of the recorded segments is that the textures are almost always continuous, with very few definitive cuts from one block to another and no silences within segments (unlike the ensemble part, where there are many scored silences).

Formal Design

Kraanerg's formal design can perhaps best be thought of as a sonic mosaic.[1] The music is made up of relatively short blocks, each defined by distinctive parameters such as instrumentation or texture. Our analysis takes Xenakis's listing of musical parameters in his early sketches as the point of departure in determining the characteristics of the mosaic materials, for the ensemble segments at least (the recorded parts are similar, but given the layering and processing, are harder to define with precision).

Each ensemble or playback segment may contain a number of blocks, distinguished by parameter shifts. As an example, the opening ensemble segment utilizes the full complement of winds, each performing a fixed pitch by means of repeated staccato articulation, each instrument entering and stopping independently (this texture strongly recalls the opening of *Akrata*, a work for winds comprised primarily of repeated staccato articulations). By "fixed pitch" is meant a single duration of staccato articulations that is usually separated by a silence before a new pitch is sounded by that instrument. At 8.5 seconds in, select instruments start to play normal sustained notes, at a lower dynamic marking (*f* instead of *fff*). While there is overlap, this shift of articulation and dynamics represents a second formal block. All the winds return to staccato articulation by 18″, but from 20.5″ the sustained

---

[1] James Harley, "Nonlinear mosaic form: Kraanerg by Iannis Xenakis," in *Proceedings of the Xenakis International Symposium Southbank Centre, London, 1–3 April 2011* (www.gold.ac.uk/media/04.2 James Harley.pdf, 2011).

Example 4.5 *Kraanerg*, opening winds segment

and staccato notes are mixed until the end of the segment at 38″. The only other parameter to vary in this segment is the pitch range, with the piccolo jumping to the extreme high register at 22″ and the 1st trombone and contrabassoon shifting to their low ranges at 21″ and 23″ respectively.

When the playback part enters with its first segment at 0′34″ (overlapping the ensemble by 4 seconds), the listener can hear a marked resemblance to the ensemble material. The winds are heard playing repeated staccato notes there as well. Of course, there are also significant differences in what one hears. Even if the material is the same, or very similar, it has been altered in the studio, using filtering, gain distortion, and so forth. In the performance, these sounds would be coming from loudspeakers around the audience, so the sound quality is also mediated by those sources, and would be separated spatially from the live ensemble.

In this analysis, "segments" are defined as the sections of music of either the live ensemble or the recorded elements that are built from "blocks" of material characterized by specific parameter qualities and combinations, namely instrumentation, register, playing mode, dynamics, density, and sonic entity. For the most part, the segments of ensemble and playback music alternate, although there are overlaps and a few concurrent segments. If one listens just for the alternation of these segments, and their durations, a basic formal outline arises. For the first 23 minutes, there is a more or less equal balance between the two. Then, at the end of the eighth playback segment, a much longer passage of ensemble music begins. The ensemble dominates, in terms of segment durations, right through to 52′00″, when the focus shifts definitively to the playback element. The final 23 minutes contains three lengthy segments of recorded music, the longest of the entire work. This shifting of balance between these basic elements of the music suggests a three-part form:

Part One	0′00″–23′00″:	balance between ensemble and playback;
Part Two	23′00″–52′00″:	ensemble dominates;
Part Three	52′00″–75′11″:	playback dominates

Furthermore, while Part One is relatively continuous, with overlapping shifts between ensemble and playback segments, Part Two features some fracturing of the extended ensemble segments, with many notable silences. Part Three is the most continuous, with the long segments of playback dominating. A more detailed discussion of the formal organization of these three large sections will follow later.

This large-scale formal shape may be difficult to perceive, given the protracted duration of the work, but these shifts of balance nonetheless have an impact on perception even while more attention may be paid to the smaller-scale play of sonic blocks within segments. A glance back at the organization of the choreography shows that there is no correlation between this tripartite musical form and the dance form as created by Petit. There is no necessity for any such correlation, of course, and from the choreographer's viewpoint, it makes good sense to place an intermission halfway through. And, even with dance "movements" involving different dancers and different dance sequences, the music nonetheless continues. As we shall see, subsequent choreographers adopted different strategies for setting this monolithic sonic mosaic to dance.

Figure 4.1 provides a graphic representation of the 24 ensemble and 20 playback segments of *Kraanerg*, showing their durations and where they overlap or sound concurrently. The playback segments display a composite amplitude waveform, giving an overall sense of dynamic energy within those segments. The ensemble segments show when woodwinds, brass, or strings are present, and provide the high and low boundaries of the pitches used in each segment as well.

For the ensemble segments, the changes of instrumentation, and the shifts of register are good indications of the inner block-structure. Figure 4.2 displays the changes of sonic entity, here modified from Xenakis's original sketches to describe the textural elements that seem most important in the final score, ordered in the diagram from bottom to top:

1. fixed pitches (relatively), sustained or articulated;
2. fluctuating sonorities (regarding pitch or possibly dynamics);
3. glissandi (they are rarely in parallel, for the most part they trace crossing trajectories);
4. mixed, complex textures (rapid changes within each instrumental line, or composite mixture).

Additional charts could track changes of the other parameters: playing mode, dynamics, and density. While this would be useful, it is sufficient to note that shifts in these parameters usually work in tandem with changes in instrumentation, register, and/or sonic entity. There are exceptions to such parametrical synchronicity, of course: the changes of the first segment, as noted above, are primarily conveyed by shifts of articulation (staccato to sustained notes) and dynamics. A more detailed discussion of the formal organization will follow below.

Electroacoustic Elements

Turning back to the playback segments, there are observations that can be made even without access to detailed information about how the material was put together. As noted earlier, Xenakis produced two 40-minute continuous strands of music recorded by the strings of the ensemble and two similar ones by the winds. The sketches indicate that this material was either taken from, or modeled on, *Akrata* (winds) and *Nomos gamma* (winds and strings, separately). Given that the instrumentation is not the same, most likely the available instruments played selected parts of the existing scores, or similar music. As Benoît Gibson has noted,

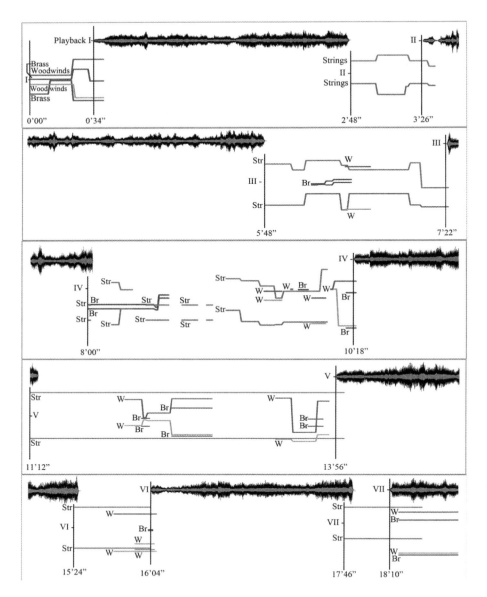

Figure 4.1   *Kraanerg*: outline of ensemble/playback segments

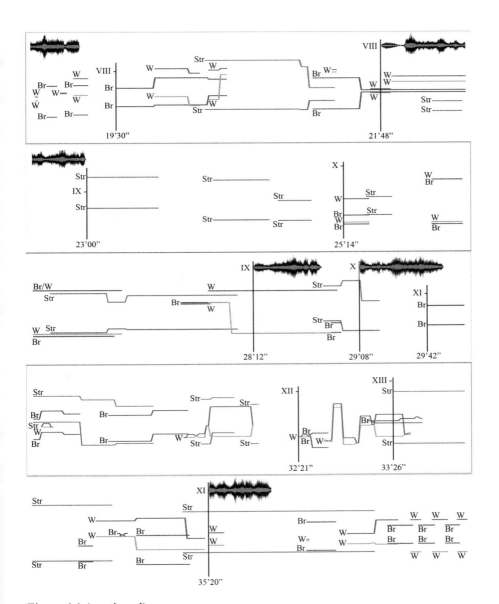

Figure 4.1 (continued)

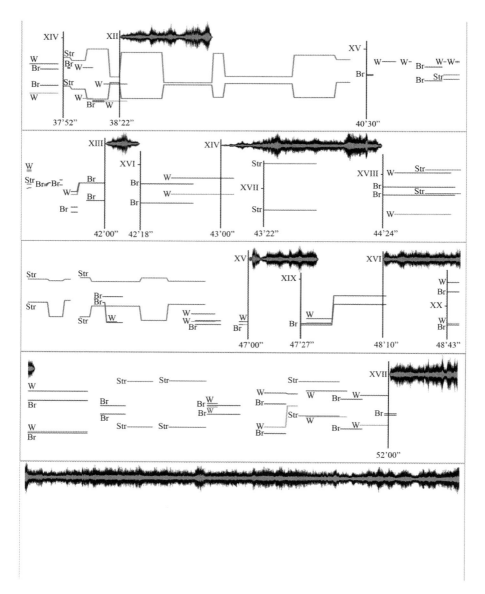

Figure 4.1 (continued)

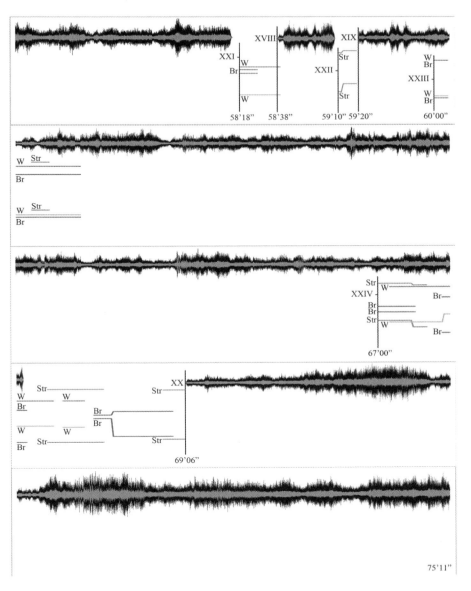

Figure 4.1 (continued)

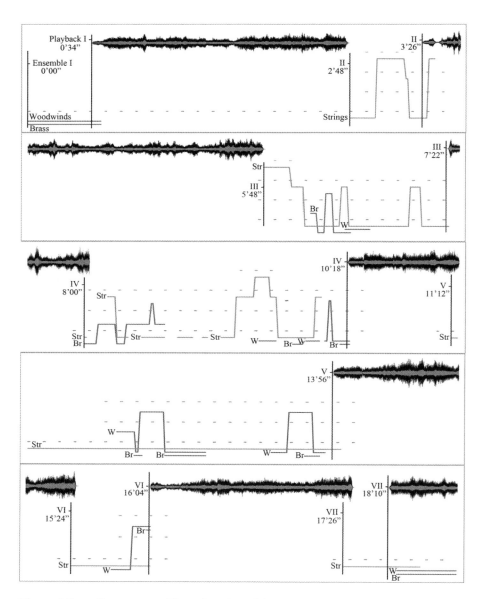

Figure 4.2 *Kraanerg*: outline of sonic entities

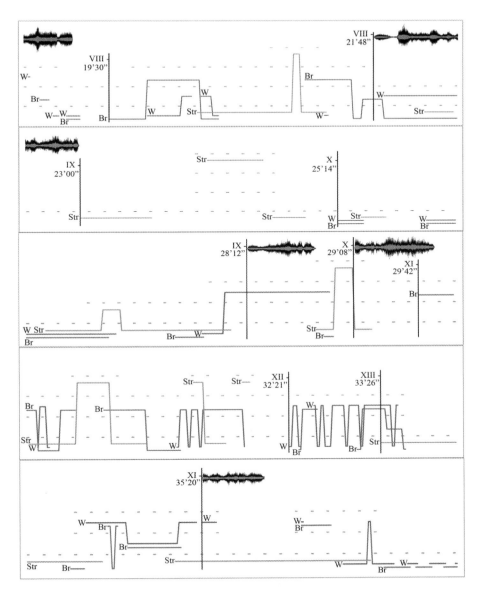

Figure 4.2 (continued)

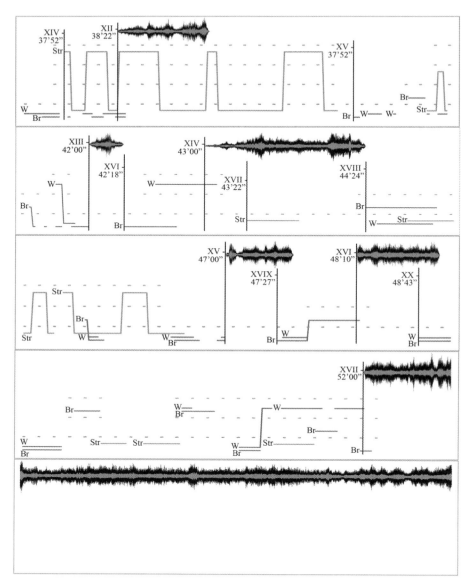

Figure 4.2 (continued)

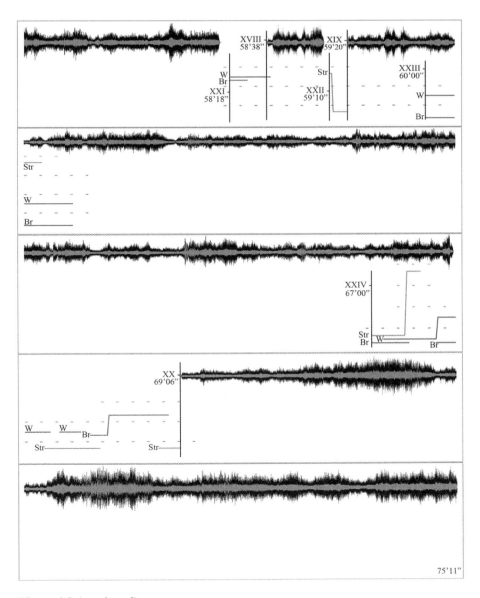

Figure 4.2 (continued)

there are also many examples in the ensemble score for *Kraanerg* that are lifted from *Nomos gamma* (and also from *Nuits*).[2]

It is worth noting that such excerpts taken from *Nomos gamma* would very likely not be recognizable in *Kraanerg*. This passage, with borrowed material taken from five individual string parts, is from a texture scored for 48 individual string parts. The ensemble material recorded in the studio may well have come from existing scores, as noted, but could be entirely unrecognizable, not only for having come from larger textures but also for the studio treatment the recordings were then subjected to. Similarly for the instrumental parts in *Kraanerg* borrowed from earlier scores: besides being extracted from much larger textures, the material does not always stand alone, being sometimes combined with other material. Existing sketches for the recorded parts do seem to indicate a plan for mixing the four layers of material (two layers of winds and two of strings) and spatializing them into four channels. More discussion on the spatialization will follow below.

The work in the studio to transform the recorded material seems to have consisted of fairly rudimentary processing, working with composite recordings of the ensembles rather than treating separate tracks of individual instruments. Xenakis appears to have been aiming for a fairly murky texture, to distinguish the playback material from the clarity of the live ensemble. One operation Xenakis used was *filtering*, to alter the overall frequency profile of the material. In other words, a recording of the winds might be filtered so that the higher frequencies of the sound are attenuated. The result would be a muffled quality. Or, the low frequencies of the strings might be attenuated so that the sound is bright and tinny, with little body. This could be used, for example, to enhance the percussive quality of tapping on the strings with the wood of the bow (a playing mode Xenakis makes much use of in *Kraanerg*). Another operation is *gain adjustment*, where the sound is run through an amplifier to boost the levels, one result being to produce a form of distortion. There is a great deal of distortion added throughout, so much so that it is rare to hear a relatively clear sonority (when it does happen, it usually involves the strings). *Reverberation* is another studio operation that can make a signal sound like it is coming from a distance, or is resonating in a large, echoing space. Reverb will also contribute to a lack of clarity in the signal, and Xenakis seems to have been more interested in this aspect of the processing than in adding artificial spatiality to the signal. He also applied *pitch alteration* to the signal at times, making it sound higher or lower (different tape speeds shift the pitch of a signal by one octave, while at the same time changing the speed by a factor of two or one-half). Tape speed changes are used sparingly, but they are most noticeable in textures that include long, low drones that could not be performed by an instrumentalist (aside from detuned strings, discussed in the section below on the Annexes). Xenakis made much more use of this form of sonic transformation in

---

[2] Benoît Gibson, *The Instrumental Music of Iannis Xenakis: Theory, Practice, Self-Borrowing* (Hillsdale, NY: Pendragon, 2011), 174–92.

Example 4.6 *Nomos gamma*: score excerpt, mm. 409–13

Example 4.7 *Kraanerg*: score excerpt showing borrowing from *Nomos gamma*, 3:02–3:18

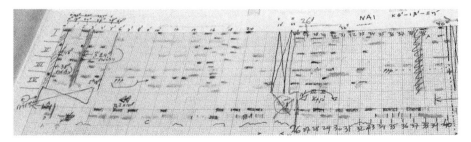

Figure 4.3   *Kraanerg*: sketch of recorded material formal plan (Xenakis Archives)

other electroacoustic works such as *Concret PH* (1958), *Bohor* (1962), or *Hibiki-Hana-Ma* (1970), where the alteration of pitch is used extensively to radically alter the material or create full-range textures from specific sources.

What Xenakis did *not* do in *Kraanerg* is to reverse the recordings so that sounds are played backwards. He also avoided editing the interior characteristics of the recorded sounds, such as cutting the attack, lifting the sustained portion, or splicing a portion of one sound onto a portion of another. As his source material is music performed by ensembles of winds and strings, he may have felt that cutting and splicing would be too drastic an operation to apply to these composite textures (however, there is a great deal of splicing in his next studio work, *Hibiki-Hana-Ma*).

The other main studio element in *Kraanerg* is the *spatialization* of the recordings, as the playback segments are intended to be heard coming from four channels surrounding the audience. Based on listening to the playback segments in isolation, and on examining the sketches, it seems most likely that Xenakis mixed the four layers separately onto a four-track tape, then combined them to produce a composite four-track recording with each layer spatialized independently. The sketch excerpt shown here uses four colored markings within each system, marked I through IV. While the sketch seems to be a preliminary one, it does indicate the composer's strategy to distribute four layers of material into the four channels (another part of the sketch provides a key to the colors, two referring to winds and two to strings). The shaded out parts at the beginning and near the 3-minute mark appear to indicate the live ensemble segments where the playback is silent.

In contrast to *Polytope de Montréal*, where the sonic material travels around the channels (or ensembles) mostly in circular fashion, the spatialization in *Kraanerg* is more complex. The other important difference from the earlier score is that the material in *Polytope de Montréal* uses time delays as well as amplitude shifts to emulate the effect of *moving* sound. In *Kraanerg*, there are no delays or timing differences between channels, so there is less an effect of sounds traveling around the channels as there is one of shifting source locations. As the graphic display of the recorded segments shows, there are times when the signal is not present in

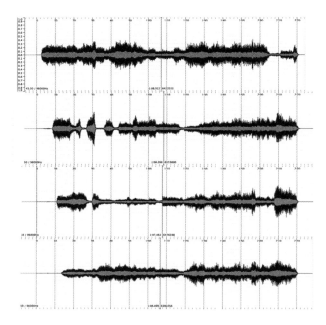

Figure 4.4 Four-channel amplitude display, Playback Segment I (0:34–2:52)

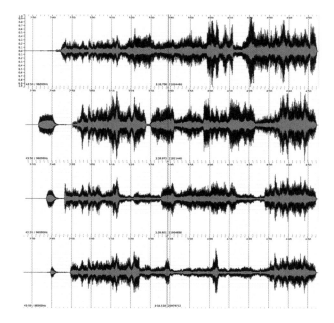

Figure 4.5 Four-channel amplitude display, Playback Segment II (3:26–5:48)

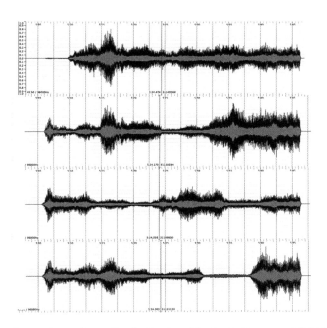

Figure 4.6   Four-channel amplitude display, Playback Segment III (7:22–8:02)

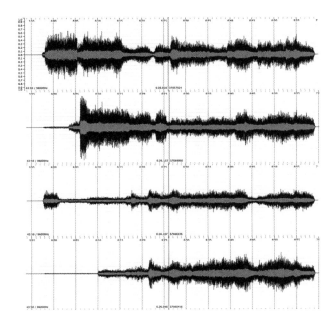

Figure 4.7   Four-channel amplitude display, Playback Segment IV (10:18–11:18)

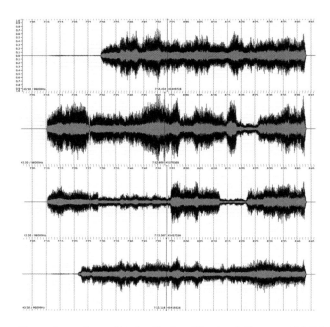

Figure 4.8　　Four-channel amplitude display, Playback Segment V (13:56–15:28)

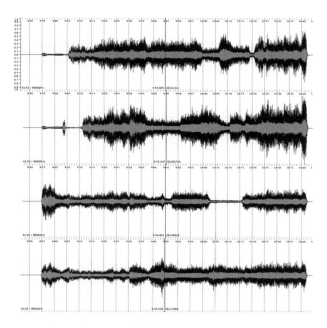

Figure 4.9　　Four-channel amplitude display, Playback Segment VI (16:04–17:50)

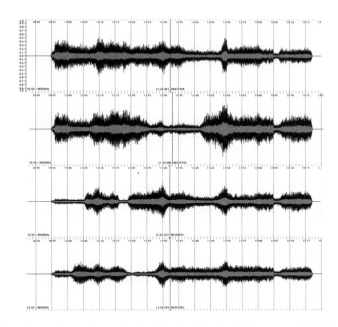

Figure 4.10　Four-channel amplitude display, Playback Segment VII (18:10–19:32)

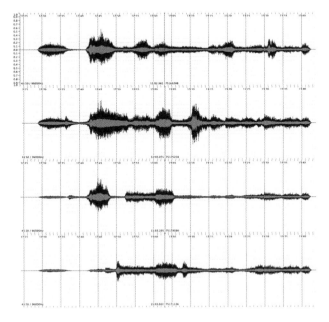

Figure 4.11　Four-channel amplitude display, Playback Segment VIII (21:48–23:00)

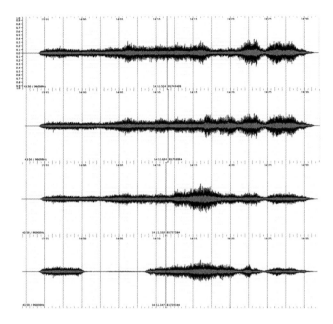

Figure 4.12 Four-channel amplitude display, Playback Segment IX (28:12–28:48)

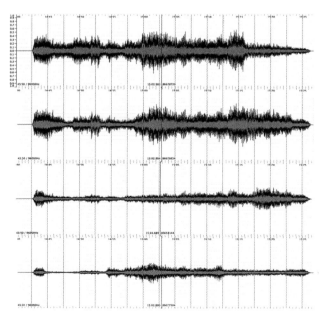

Figure 4.13 Four-channel amplitude display, Playback Segment X (29:08–29:50)

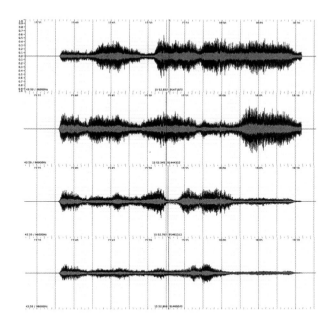

Figure 4.14   Four-channel amplitude display, Playback Segment XI (35:20–35:52)

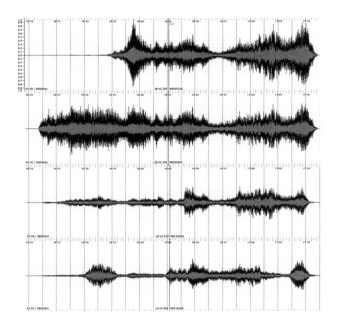

Figure 4.15   Four-channel amplitude display, Playback Segment XII (38:22–39:10)

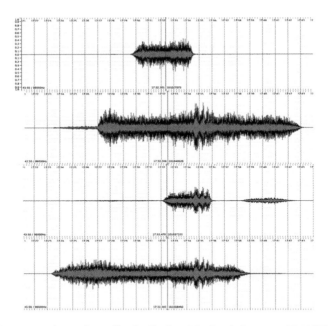

Figure 4.16 Four-channel amplitude display, Playback Segment XIII (42:00–42:18)

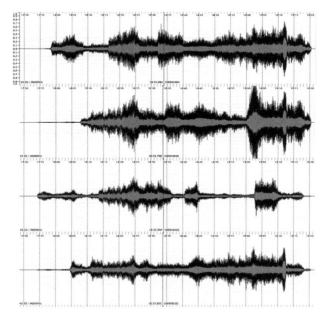

Figure 4.17 Four-channel amplitude display, Playback Segment XIV (43:00–44:22)

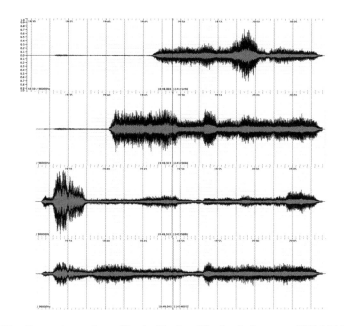

Figure 4.18   Four-channel amplitude display, Playback Segment XV (47:00–47:36)

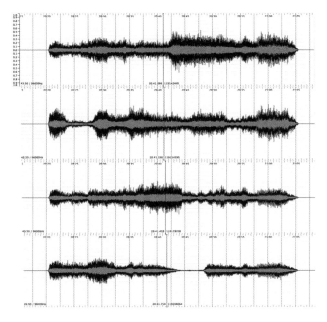

Figure 4.19   Four-channel amplitude display, Playback Segment XVI (48:10–48:54)

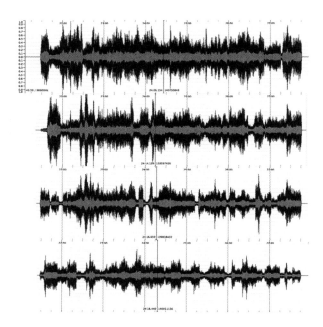

Figure 4.20   Four-channel amplitude display, Playback Segment XVII (52:00–58:24)

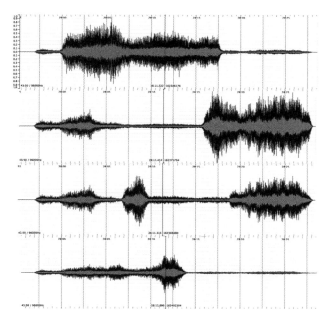

Figure 4.21   Four-channel amplitude display, Playback Segment XVIII (58:38–59:10)

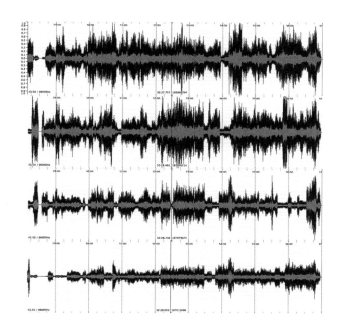

Figure 4.22   Four-channel amplitude display, Playback Segment XIX (59:20–67:42)

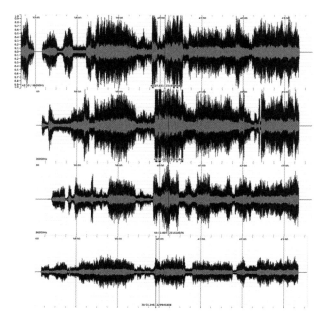

Figure 4.23   Four-channel amplitude display, Playback Segment XX (69:06–75:11)

one or more channels; but more often there are differences of amplitude, subtle or significant, between them as the mix creates a sense of shifting spatial presence for the playback.

These amplitude displays of the four channels of playback material show, at least globally, that the spatialization strategy in *Kraanerg* is sophisticated. If, as we conjecture, the four layers of material were mixed separately onto the four-track tape, the distribution of the sounds around the channels would be complex, with one of the layers being prominent in one (or more) channels for a period of time while another layer could be more prominent in another channel, and so on. Careful listening to the playback segments confirms this as the most likely strategy. One result of this sophisticated approach to mixing would have been to render live intervention or balancing ("diffusion") by a sound technician unnecessary. The composer was not interested in relegating control to a mix performer, so all he required was a good sound system and one or more four-track tape machines. This was a prudent strategy given the intention of the National Ballet of Canada to tour the work. Dance theaters at the time would have had little (or no) need for a high-quality, multi-channel sound system.

It is worth noting that the other strategy for multi-channel sound one could adopt, that of placing distinct sounds into different channels independently of each other, is something Xenakis avoids in *Kraanerg*. Given the restricted material he was working with (recorded ensembles of winds and strings), and the severe time constraints he was operating under, such a decision was understandable. This approach did, however, become a fundamental strategy for all his subsequent multi-channel works, beginning with *Hibiki-Hana-Ma* and including *Persepolis, Polytope de Cluny*, and *La légende d'Eer*. In these works, different layers of material, derived from a wide range of sources and carrying often quite contrasting sonic characteristics, are placed into different channels so they are heard as originating from unique locations. The sounds do not move (there may be some movement of layers to different channels, depending on the piece), but delineate a rich sonic space, along the lines of natural soundscapes.

Formal Plan

Returning to the organization of *Kraanerg* as a whole, Table 4.1 summarizes the ensemble and playback segments, their start times, their durations, and the time interval between the end of a segment and the start of the next one (of the same category, ensemble, or playback).

The average duration of all the segments is 104″, not far off Xenakis's early estimation of 107″, when he was figuring on 42 segments. Taken separately, the playback segments are on average longer (117′) and the ensemble segments shorter (93″). This is logical given that there are four more ensemble segments than playback ones. There is a wide variation in segment durations, from 10″ to

Table 4.1   Timing of segments in *Kraanerg*

Ensemble segment	Playback segment	Start time	Duration (seconds)	Interval (between segments)
		Part One		
I		0:00	38	(130)
	I	0:34	138	(34)
II		2:48	42	(138)
	II	3:26	142	(94)
III		5:48	96	(36)
	III	7:22	40	(136)
IV		8:00	140	(52)
	IV	10:18	60	(158)
V		11:12	168	(84)
	V	13:56	92	(36)
VI		15:24	42	(100)
	VI	16:04	106	(20)
VII		17:46	90	(14)
	VII	18:10	82	(136)
VIII		19:30	182	(28)
	VIII	21:48	72	(312)
		Part Two		
IX		23:00	118	(16)
X		25:14	244	(24)
	IX	28:12	36	(20)
	X	29:08	42	(330)
XI		29:42	138	(21)
XII		32:21	65	(0)
XIII		33:26	264.5	(1.5)
	XI	35:20	32	(150)
XIV		37:52	150	(8)
	XII	38:22	48	(170)
XV		40:30	90	(18)
	XIII	42:00	18	(42)
XVI		42:18	49	(15)
	XIV	43:00	84	(156)
XVII		43:22	28	(34)
XVIII		44:24	156	(26)
	XV	47:00	36	(34)
XIX		47:27	45	(31)
	XVI	48:10	44	(186)
XX		48:43	201	(374)

Table 4.1 continued

Ensemble segment	Playback segment	Start time	Duration (seconds)	Interval (between segments)
		Part Three		
	XVII	52:00	384	(14)
XXI		58:18	22	(30)
	XVIII	58:38	32	(10)
XXII		59:10	10	(40)
	XIX	59:20	502	(84)
XXIII		60:00	42	(378)
XXIV		67:00	126	(365)
	XX	69:06	365	end

502″, and the largest close-range cluster of durations is found between 28″ and 49″, encompassing 15 segments. While generally there is a balance between ensemble and playback in terms of segment durations, the one significant distinction is in the longest segments. While the ensemble material includes one segment that is 264.5″ and another that is 244″, the next longest segment is significantly shorter, at 182″. By contrast, the longest playback segment is 502″, almost twice the duration of the longest ensemble segment. There are two other playback segments significantly longer than the longest ensemble segment as well: 384″ and 365″. So, while overall, the ensemble and playback elements balance each other, these durational differences contribute to the contrasting aspects of these elements. We have already noted that the playback material is more continuous, with four layers of recorded sound being mixed together to produce a generally denser, more sustained texture. The clearer, more defined sonorities heard in the live ensemble support sharper shifts of texture, and a rather dramatic use of silence within segments. The shifting blocks of material within the ensemble segments at times make it difficult to determine whether the segment continues or whether a new one starts. Xenakis exploits this formal–perceptual ambiguity several times in *Kraanerg*, especially in the middle part of the work where the ensemble dominates and where there are many silences inserted into the score. Ultimately, for the listener, the distinction between new segment and new block is not all that important. The momentum that drives the work comes from the interaction between these structural levels, their changing durations and sound qualities, and the play of shifting parameters such as instrumentation, register, sonic entity, and so forth.

The mosaic-like quality of the music has a kaleidoscopic character, as elements are perpetually shuffled and renewed. There are few moments of strikingly new material in *Kraanerg*, beyond the initial passages, but if a sonic entity such as a glissando is presented for the first time with a reduced density, say for a solo instrument, it will nonetheless be notable for being a new presentation of a familiar gesture that may have been heard earlier with the whole string section, for example. The combinatorial nature of Xenakis's compositional technique based on group theory lies at the heart of his mature style. *Kraanerg* demonstrates a less systematic approach to the theory than the earlier *Nomos alpha*, but nonetheless operates in a similar way. That is, defined musical parameters are varied in combination with each other to produce a nonlinear form in ways that enable the composer's intuition to play a strong role in the process rather than simply following a rule-bound procedure or algorithm.

Analysis

The discussion that follows is intended to provide an overview of *Kraanerg* that builds on the analysis that is demonstrated in the formal charts provided above. For the sake of convenience, we will bind the discussion within the three-part division of the work already mentioned.

Part One: 0:00–23:00

Kraanerg begins with a stretch of clear alternations between the live ensemble and the playback material. In Part One, there are eight segments of each, and the variety of musical material introduced in them significantly defines the sonic scope of the whole work. Ensemble Segment (ES) I features the winds (playing essentially fixed pitches, alternating between staccato and sustained articulations), while ES II brings in the strings alone. The sustained natural harmonics texture that opens this segment is prominent throughout *Kraanerg*, and in this segment it is interrupted twice by a densely active texture mixing pizzicati, trills, col legno battuto (tapping on the strings with the wood of the bow), tremolo, glissandi, rhythmicized harmonics, and bowed melodic fragments. Playback Segment (PS) I begins with similar material to the opening winds in ES I, but later the strings are heard; and in fact all playback segments contain two layers of processed winds and strings sounds, varyingly present in the four channels. The material in the playback segments varies, as do the segment durations, but there is a continuity between them that creates a relatively consistent identity that is less present in the ensemble segments. It is notable, nonetheless, that PS II begins with string sounds most prominently, establishing a connection with ES II. In the rest of *Kraanerg*, such connections are usually less direct.

The opening playback segments are significantly longer than the ensemble segments, but this shifts over the course of Part One, so that the ensemble segments get longer and the playback segments get shorter, overall. The end of PS II does not overlap with the start of ES III, the only time in Part One where an overlap does not happen. The effect is rather brusque, particularly as the recorded material has no fading in or out but quickly cuts off at the end of each segment. In addition, there is no overlap of common textures between the closing of the playback and launch of the ensemble segment. ES III includes both winds and strings, but they seem to have separate presences, the material for each not obviously relating to the other. The strings are present for the full segment, again alternating between dense, active blocks and sustained natural harmonics. The sixth, final block in the strings is new, consisting of clouds of percussive sounds achieved by col legno battuto. The winds appear in the middle of the segment, and are present for just 32". The winds carry on the fixed-pitch texture (sustained) from ES I, with a few fluctuations in the brass of neighboring tones or glissandi. In this case, the brass launch the block, in the middle register, then pass it on to the woodwinds, emphasizing the extremes of high and low. PS III is much briefer than the earlier segments, and is soon taken over by the ensemble in an even more extended segment, lasting 2'20". The end of ES III, with the percussive battuto texture, contrasts sharply with the much more sustained sound of PS III (although this segment ends with a layer of percussive string sounds taking prominence).

ES IV is significant for introducing the first silences of the piece and the first reduced-density textures. Continuity with ES III is established in the strings with one measure of the same battuto material (literally cut and pasted into the score at 8:00). This percussive texture makes four appearances in this segment, intercut with the complex active blocks from earlier or in combination with bowed harmonics. There are five gaps between string blocks, and three of them occur when the winds are not sounding, resulting in silences of 6", 4", and 6" in the middle of this segment. In the meantime, the winds sound only at the beginning and end of this segment. The static, staccato opening in the brass evolves into mixed articulations with neighbor-tone pitch movement. At 8:08 the density drops, leaving a solo trombone carrying on. This passage, which continues through 8:42, is one of the more substantial solo passages in the work, although the strings do cut in and out underneath the trombone, providing a percussive, textural backdrop to the more direct expression of the solo. At 9:32, the oboe picks up where the trombone leaves off, shifting to the high register. The oboe carries on to the end of the segment, with sustained notes heard sporadically in other wind instruments, in varying density.

PS IV is relatively brief, at 60", presenting primarily sustained strings with winds entering later along with a layer of percussive strings again. This segment is succeeded by the even longer ES V segment. The strings are present throughout, playing sustained double-stops (not harmonics, this time) with much fluctuation of dynamics ranging from *pp* to *fff*. While Xenakis uses quarter-tones throughout *Kraanerg*, this segment includes third-tones (the foreword to the score neglects to mention this possibility, but the composer had introduced third-tones in earlier scores, such as *Medea*). One can conjecture that Xenakis was interested in subtle variations of vibration arising from such minute intervallic changes within a thick, sustained texture. The winds blocks begin at 12:04, with microtonal melodic phrases that are passed along, overlapping, from piccolo down through the other woodwinds, carrying on the lower density from ES IV. The second winds block returns to the full-density sustained/repeated note material from earlier, this time emphasizing high and low registers, while the third block, starting at 13:24, returns to lower density, although the melodic phrases here are replaced by sustained notes articulated with accents, staccato repetitions, or flutter-tonguing. A longer passage of narrow-range glissandi in the contrabassoon provides an interlude, supported by a soft, sustained quilisma cluster in the brass. The winds drop out before the strings, where the density is gradually decreased to the end of the segment as the higher strings drop out.

PS V is more substantial again, at 92", and overlaps into ES VI, which picks up exactly where ES V left off, with low-register sustained material in the strings. The texture is again entirely sustained, but plays with density and register. In the winds, the soloistic density reappears, featuring the contrabass clarinet and contrabassoon animating sustained notes with dramatic dynamic fluctuations. PS VI is longer than the previous segment, at 106", and at first picks up the sustained texture of ES VI, then brings in other layers as it goes on. The sustained strings sound filtered and tinny, although there is also a low, diffuse drone layer that balances the high-frequency emphasis of the strings.

The first half of ES VII again features sustained strings, this time building up a 24-note sonority (each instrument playing double stops) of intense vibrations caused by close-range intervals, enhanced by layers of dynamic fluctuations between *pp* and *sfff*. At 18:10, PS VII enters while the ensemble carries on, heightening the density of the string texture with the addition of the recorded layers. Soon after the playback entry, the winds join in, playing pulsing repeated notes that sound at a slower rate than in earlier blocks, here creating notable cross rhythms through duple and triplet beat divisions. At 18:28 the strings drop out while the winds carry on along with the playback textures. There are four breaks cut into the winds blocks (the playback segment continues, however), and Xenakis uses those spaces to cut in contrasting fragments: a solo glissando in the contrabass clarinet; legato pulsations in the brass; another solo moment featuring an articulated sustained tone in the contrabass bassoon; and a wide-register sustained chord in all the winds with pulsating dynamic decays.

PS VII carries on until 19:32, overlapping with ES VIII. This segment, the longest ensemble segment of Part One, is built from nine blocks of material in the winds and five in the strings. The brass section opens this segment with a sustained unison in the middle register (but a high range for the trombones) that is varied by dynamic fluctuations around *mf* and narrow quilisma around the central pitch (a similar brass unison in the same range opens *Aïs* for baritone voice, percussion, and orchestra from 1980). A shift to a cluster chord builds from *p* to *f* then moves into an extended passage of meandering glissandi, punctuated by short notes in the woodwinds. This passage overlaps the entry of the strings at 20:16. While the strings sustain another vibrating sonority of third-tone pitches spread across the full register, the winds shift through a couple of textural blocks, the first being an intense *ffff* cluster, with low-density melodic phrases in the woodwinds, followed by a lower-range brass chord played flutter-tongue tracing a long crescendo to a cut-off at 20:28. The strings carry on until a shift of harmony at 20:44 that is underscored by a synchronization of the dynamic fluctuations and a drop in register. A brief outburst of the fast, mixed string texture introduced in ES II gives way to a new string sonority, a harsh tremolo (achieved by using stronger than normal bow pressure on the strings) at full volume. At 21:12 the block of brass glissandi with occasional woodwind punctuations returns over the top of the noisy strings before they cut out at 21:24. At 21:37 the brass land on another unison, roughened by neighboring pitches. A narrow-range legato melody in a solo horn emerges from this texture, and is picked up by the oboe, shifting to a higher register (a similar progression as occurred in ES IV). The narrow-range oboe melody continues to the end of the segment, over the roughened unison in the brass, ramped back to a very soft *ppp* with occasional loud accents. The low strings enter at 22:14, picking up the sustained chords heard earlier. In the meantime, PS VIII enters at 21:48 in parallel with the ensemble, carrying on when the ensemble drops out to close off Part One. This segment begins with a short appearance in one of the winds layers of what sounds like a high solo piccolo or oboe, heavily distorted. This sonority interacts with the oboe solo in the live ensemble, and is a rare moment in all the playback segments where a solo sonority is perceivable.

Part Two: 23:00–52:00

Where the balance between ensemble and playback elements is quite equal in Part One, and the alternation between them orderly, Part Two marks a definitive shift to give prominence to the live ensemble. From the end of PS VIII, which marks the conclusion of Part One, there is a gap of over 5 minutes to the entrance of PS IX. Part Two contains many silences, where segment blocks are set apart from each other with no other layers of sound going on to mask the separations. In ES IX, made up of three large blocks of string material, the first block, a texture of natural harmonics picking up from ES II, is followed by a 28″ silence. The second block, an extended passage of very active, mixed elements, first introduced in ES II, is then followed by a silence of 4″. The third block, low-register sustained sonorities animated by synchronized dynamic fluctuations, is followed by a 16″ silence. By this point, the listener may develop a perception of the silences as a significant structural entity. At other times (most times), the blocks of material in the ensemble segments are pasted into the score, usually separated by a space, and the silence of those spaces is covered by the overlap of sonic blocks in the other section, winds or strings, and occasionally by the additional presence of the playback element. These moments where there is nothing covering the spaces between blocks are really no different, structurally, but the effect on the listener is certainly different, given that silences in music, especially extended ones, are so rare.

After the third silence following blocks of string material, the winds enter, and the shift of sonority is significant enough to call this a new segment. So, ES X begins with two short blocks in the winds, the first being the now-familiar repeated-note fixed-pitch sonority, this time varied by layering the pulsations to create cross rhythms (similar to one of the brass blocks in ES VII, but at a faster rate). This shifts with no break to a low-register sustained sonority, roughened with flutter-tongue. The strings enter at 25:26, overlapping the winds slightly, picking up the sustained block that ended ES IX. A crescendo leads to a variant of the sustained texture, with eighth-tone neighbor pitches adding vibrational intensity to the sonority. A 20″ silence leads to a continuation of the growling low sonority in the winds, with high-register held tones in the upper woodwinds, also roughened with flutter-tongue. This winds block is lengthy, carrying on for over 1 minute, until 27:04. In the meantime, the strings are cut in again, picking up the eighth-tone sonority at 26:24. This continues, with occasional changes of pitch in individual parts, until a synchronized shift to an upper-register chord at 26:44, the eighth-tones being dropped in favor of third-tones. This block then carries on for over 1 minute, cutting off at 28:04. The sustained texture is animated by distributed accents in individual parts, with some changes of pitch as well. At 27:34, as the strings continue, the first winds block of staccato repeated notes returns, this time with the density reduced to just the two trombones. At 27:48 the woodwinds take over; then, at 28:00, a block of woodwind glissandi enters, beginning with solo piccolo, passing off to the E♭ clarinet, then bringing all five woodwinds in for a long stretch that lasts until 28:54. The grinding tremolo string sonority first heard in ES VIII returns at 28:06 for 14″, bridging the entrance of PS IX at 28:12.

    The playback element in this segment is diffuse, acting like a textural support to the woodwinds, and is brief, dropping out again at 28:48. The woodwinds continue for a little longer, and the strings enter, as PS IX finishes, with three blocks to finish out ES X. The first is a sustained sonority combining natural harmonics with grinding tremolos. This block shifts to the complex mixed texture already heard a number of times, then to a final block of percussive battuto, each string layer shifting between duplet, triplet, and quintuplet beat divisions to create a complex cloud of attacks.

    PS X, entering at 29:08 to overlap with the final strings block of ES X, provides a brief interlude before the longest stretch of ensemble music with no playback, comprising three segments presented back-to-back. PS XI is brief, just 32″, and is heard in the middle of ES XIII, which then carries on for another 2 minutes. PS XII is also brief, and is also only heard concurrently with ES XIV, which carries through on its own, leading to the next ensemble segment. An autonomous playback segment is not heard until 42:00, when PS XIII takes over from ES XV.

    ES XI is constructed from seven blocks in the winds and six in the strings. The segment begins at 29:42 with brass section glissandi, transferred over from the woodwinds in ES X. This texture continues for 25″ then lands on a held flutter-tongue harmony, quickly shifting to a higher-range sustained sonority, the flutter-tongue replaced by rapid dynamic fluctuations to create an amplitude-modulation effect. At 30:19 the brass shift back into glissandi, cut off at 30:24 but starting up again at 30:42. In the meantime, the strings enter at 30:02, picking up the grinding tremolo texture last heard as the first block of ES X. This block continues beyond the cut-off of the brass, shifting at 30:28 to a complex mixed sonority (the second block in ES X), then to a composite texture of high held pitches, with eighth-tone neighbor tones, and battuto (carrying on the layered divisions from the end of ES X). The brass glissandi start up again while the strings are still in their second block (mixed sonority). As the strings stop, the brass move to held tones varied by quilisma and amplitude fluctuations, as was heard in ES VIII (Part One), here sounding a narrow-range mid-register chord rather than a unison. The brass are succeeded, with a brief overlap, by the low woodwinds playing staccato repeated notes, varied with narrow-range glissandi, flutter-tongue, and dramatic dynamic modulations. The strings enter at 31:30 with a strong outburst of the mixed texture, shifting to the composite sonority comprising sustained natural harmonics and grinding tremoli. As the strings shift to this new block, the upper woodwinds take over from the lower instruments, then all five instruments join in to end the block. As the woodwinds are finishing, the strings, dropped at 31:48, cut in with a short 4" passage of the complex mixed texture heard earlier in the segment.

After a 21" silence ES XII begins, and could arguably be understood as a continuation of ES XI, given the shared material. However, even though the winds start the segment with the same staccato/glissando/flutter-tongue phrases as end the winds blocks in ES XI, the density is lower when the winds enter, the brass are brought into the texture, and the strings are barely present. The contrabass clarinet begins the segment, overlapping a solo horn, in turn overlapping a trombone, then moving to contrabassoon. Given how rare such low-density moments are in *Kraanerg*, the solo line after a lengthy silence is a significant segment marker. This winds block continues throughout the segment, with varying densities and occasional punctuations in the high woodwinds. This ability to cast new light on existing material by varying the density demonstrates the power of Xenakis's "group theory" approach to composition. As ES XII finishes off, the accented sustained notes in the low strings that enter at 33:10 are secondary to the winds, but do provide a kind of diffuse low drone that is similar to what is often heard in the playback material.

Without a break, ES XIII begins at 33:26 with a full-range 24-note sonority in the strings, a dramatic textural shift from the previous segment featuring overlapping solo winds. This segment is the longest of all the ensemble segments, at well over 4 minutes, and the strings exceptionally stick to single texture, sustained bowed harmonies, throughout. What varies is the density, the register, the rate, and synchronization of the accents. In addition, Xenakis cuts a silence into the string texture, from 34:30 to 35:06. The seven winds blocks contain a wider range of material. The long opening passage for strings alone drops its density to just the double basses at 34:10, joined 2 seconds later by the horns then the rest of the brass playing flutter-tongue low-register notes at high volume. This block quickly breaks off, though, shifting to a long, solo glissando line in the E♭ clarinet, passing off to the oboe that is then joined by trumpets, all at soft dynamic levels. The strings cut out at 34:30, in the midst of the glissando texture in the winds, leaving an exposed low-density sonority. At 34:44 there is a sudden shift to a full-density winds block, a contrapuntal passage played legato at full volume. This passage is very simple, rhythmically, and sounds like an exercise in 11-part first- or second-species counterpoint (although the melodic lines do include quarter-tones). This is new material in *Kraanerg*, and a texture Xenakis would make much use of in numerous orchestral scores in the 1980s and 1990s.

At 35:06, as the winds block begins to wrap up, instruments dropping out at different points, the strings enter again, picking up where they left off. The winds return to the overlapping solo glissando phrases of ES XII, beginning with contrabass clarinet and contrabassoon (mid-register). At 35:20, as this block continues, PS XI comes in, filling out the texture for a brief 32″, adding grittiness to the overall sonority primarily with a variety of string textures. The ensemble strings continue after the playback element drops out, and the winds enter again at 36:10. The first block here is the full brass section playing glissandi, this time enhanced with flutter-tonguing. The next block features the two clarinets playing quiet held tones tuned a quarter-tone apart, eventually expanding outward by means of diverging glissandi. A shift to higher dynamics and flutter-tongue leads to a held chord of all wind instruments, quiet with an accented cut-off. This gesture of held tones with *sfff* cut-offs is continued, passing around pairs or trios of winds. The full section is brought back in to finish the segment.

The brief silence that follows ES XIII is the spot where Roland Petit decided to insert the intermission for his setting of *Kraanerg*. The dramatic cut-offs of the held chords in the winds could perhaps be thought of as cadential, although the score for the winds continues, an indication that Xenakis did not think of the material to follow as a new segment. Be that as it may, the strings do cut in at 37:52, launching into the complex, mixed texture heard before, marked *fff*. For this reason, we call this the start of ES XIV, another lengthy segment formed of 10 string blocks alternating between the complex mixed texture, battuto (sometimes in combination with grinding sounds), and pizzicato (repeated notes, layered rhythms). The final block is bowed natural harmonics. The winds are little present in ES XIV, one 6″ block of staccato repeated notes in the woodwinds, followed by a second block of low-register held tones in either brass or low woodwinds, either flutter-tongue or normal. The end of the winds block at 38:26 overlaps with PS XII, entering at 38:22 and continuing until 39:10, the cut-off also marked by a shift in the ensemble strings from a pizzicato block to the mixed texture. The playback element is mostly made up of sustained textures, primarily strings and high woodwinds, with low drones that are less prominent, all distorted in comparison with the live ensemble strings.

ES XV contains a number of silences cut into the segment blocks, hearkening back to ES IX at the beginning of Part Two. In addition to the 8″ silence that separates ES XIV from ES XV, there are six other silences in this segment: 4″, 6″, 7″, 6″, 4″, 4″, respectively. ES XV features the winds in varying lower-density combinations. There is no point in this segment where the full complement of winds plays together, unusually. The first short block features a trumpet and trombone alternating short notes marked "like a pizzicato." A silence leads to a solo featuring a high held note in the E♭ clarinet, elaborated with dynamic changes, accents, and a shift to flutter-tongue. The clarinet is cut off by a silence, then carries on briefly before another break. A shift back to the "pizzicato" short notes in the brass is filled out by both trumpets and trombones. With no break, this block shifts back to the E♭ clarinet (playing the same pitch), this time joined by a solo cello playing the same pitch as a harmonic but distorted through sul ponticello, tremolo and trilling, along with accents and rapid dynamic fluctuations. The clarinet, too, begins to distort its tone in this passage, with rapid dynamic fluctuations and quilisma. This passage is significant for being the only "duo" combining a wind and a string instrument. The combination of clarinet and cello is one Xenakis returned to soon after completing *Kraanerg* in his short, but intense, duo, *Charisma*, from 1971.

Another silence leads to a return of the brass "pizzicato," this time just two players, like the first time. Another silence cuts this off after 4″, followed by a continuation, even shorter, cut off again by a final silence. The concluding passage of this segment contains three short blocks. The first is striking for the sonorous low-register perfect fifth interval sounding in the horns and trombones, with the oboe doubling the bottom note two octaves higher, then bending it upward with a glissando. As the brass and oboe die away the piccolo enters, sustaining a high-register pitch that, while reminiscent of the earlier blocks featuring the E♭ clarinet, also happens to be the major third of the chord implied by the low-register interval in the brass. This harmonious moment is shattered by the final block that cuts to forceful held tones in all the brass, sounding unrelated pitches including quarter-tones, and rotating amongst staccato repetitions, flutter-tongue, and normal sustained tones. The brass are cut off at 42:00 by PS XIII, which launches in with no overlap. This is the shortest of all the playback segments, just 18″, but it does take the attention away from the live ensemble for the first time since PS X, more than 12 minutes earlier in the piece. In spite of its brevity, there is a lot of sonic activity in PS XIII, with all four layers present and audible.

There is no overlap between PS XIII and ES XVI, which starts in at 42:18. This segment again features the brass, and in fact picks up the sustained brass texture that ended ES XV. This block overlaps the second one, which features the high woodwinds playing a counterpoint of mostly legato melodic phrases, all marked glissandi, occasionally disturbed by a flutter-tongue note. The dynamic swells range between *p* and *fff*. The pitch range of this passage stays mid-high register, the final piccolo phrase sliding up into the extreme high register to end. PS XIV overlaps the high woodwinds, and it is possible to pick out high notes in the recorded woodwinds along with other layers such as battuto strings to convey continuity between the ensemble and playback segments here.

Unusually, PS XIV continues right through ES XVII, only stopping at the start of ES XVIII. The sustained strings that featured throughout ES XIII are picked up again in ES XVII, although in this short segment the density does not vary. Xenakis uses third-tones at first, then shifts to quarter-tones for the final two harmonies. PS

XIV carries on for another 34" after the end of the strings in ES XVII, and by now one can sense the balance between the ensemble and the playback elements shifting.

ES XVIII is nonetheless quite substantial. There are five blocks of winds presenting three distinct textures (with silences cut into them), primarily featuring the brass. There are seven blocks in the strings, again presenting three textures. The segment opens at 44:24 with the brass taking over from PS XIV. The full brass section sounds an individually rotating mixture of mid-register held tones, played either flutter-tongue, quilisma, repeated staccato, or rapid dynamic fluctuations, alternating with narrow-range melodic passages played staccato. The general dynamic marking is *fff*, with some notes/phrases played *mf*. In the first block, which lasts until 45:02, the upper woodwinds contribute long, high-register notes, each shaped by a lengthy crescendo-decrescendo from *pp* to *fff* and back. At 44:46 the strings enter with sustained natural harmonics, carrying on after the winds are cut off. At 45:16 the strings shift to the familiar mixed texture, densely active, then quickly shift back again to the harmonics. Another such shift occurs at 45:32, then, after 6", the strings jump to a different sustained texture, this time playing detuned double-stop unisons. While this fifth block is sounding in the strings, the winds enter at 45:32, the brass briefly carrying on the same texture as before, but finishing with sustained tones that incrementally fade out to leave a unison note in the trombones. At 46:04, after the winds have dropped out, the strings shift back again to the mixed texture, then return to the detuned unisons until they are cut off at 46:38. Just prior, at 46:30, the brass and low woodwinds enter with varied sustained tones as before, this time with a lower density and without the melodic phrases. An 8" silence is cut into this block, which picks right up again for 6" to end the segment.

PS XV takes over at 47:00, and, in spite of its brevity, is an active segment, with battuto strings, string harmonics and dense mixed passages, low brass, high woodwinds, etc. ES XIX takes over at 47:27 and features the winds entirely. This brief segment is formed of two blocks. The first is comprised of low-register flutter-tongue held tones, passed around the horns, trombones, and low woodwinds. The second block, beginning at 47:44 without break, features the two horns playing narrow phrases in a two-part counterpoint that is complicated by occasional flutter-tongue notes, strong accents, and quarter-tones. PS XVI takes over from the horns at 48:10, the prominent filtered strings that launch the segment contrasting strongly with the middle-register activity of the brass. This segment is again relatively brief, and overlaps by 12" the start of ES XX. The complex layering of sounds in PS XVI causes the focused sound of the sustained winds chord that begins the ensemble segment to stand out.

ES XX is one of the most substantial segments for the live ensemble, and it closes off Part Two. This segment is the last to have silences cut into it, in this case three times. The opening is a substantial block for winds, with the whole section playing a held harmony (which changes once), spread across the full register, at a marking of *fff*. The sustained texture is enhanced with flutter-tongue interventions, at first in the E♭ clarinet, then the trumpets, and so on. A 7" silence at 49:21 is followed not by a continuation of the same texture but by a shift to long glissandi in the brass. At 49:42 the brass are displaced by the strings, the full group playing sustained, occasionally accented double stops, a texture that hearkens back to ES XVII and ES XIII. An 8″ silence is inserted into this material, which picks up again where it left off.

The strings carry on until 50:24 when the winds take over. Here, the brass carry on the long glissandi from the previous block, and the high woodwinds add a brief layer of more active material similar to the horns at 47:44 in the previous segment. The two horns carry on the glissando texture after the other brass drop out, followed by a third silence at 50:42. Following a 12″ break, the full winds enter on another sustained harmony, this time animated by staccato repeated notes. At 51:06 the staccato repeated notes are followed by melodic phrases in the upper woodwinds, played "quasi glissando." A break in this texture signals the entrance of the strings, continuing the sustained material from before. The upper woodwinds pick up the glissando melodies, joined by the lower woodwinds as well. An interruption of loud held tones in the brass, playing either normally, repeated staccato, or flutter-tongue, signals the end of the strings block, but gives way to the woodwinds at 51:44, who carry on until 52:00, the entrance of PS XVII. At the very end of the winds block, the two horns play legato repeated notes as a transition into the playback material.

Part Three: 52:00–75:11

There is no clear break to mark the beginning of Part Three, but the structural shift is clear as PS XVII carries on for over 6 minutes with no ensemble interventions. In all of Part Two, the longest section of the work, the playback element is only briefly present, the longest segment being 84″, and three of the playback segments occurring concurrently with the ensemble. The extended duration of PS XVII enables the audience to settle in to listen to the spatialization of the music that surrounds them, and to follow the play of the four layers of material, as different elements arise and are then subsumed by others. There is also more time to focus on the coloration of the processing, affecting in particular the low, rumbling drones that are mostly indistinct, and the grating character of the battuto strings. Perhaps more important for the listener is the time and space presented in this segment to take in the numerous textural shifts. In earlier, especially the shorter, playback segments, one is especially influenced by the general contrasts from the ensemble segments, noting the layering and sense of continuity, with no sharp breaks or silences. In PS XVII, there are some fairly sharp shifts of texture that stand out, with occasional brute cuts of material in one layer or another. One also has time to notice the similarities between sonic blocks in the playback material and previously heard blocks in the ensemble segments. The end of PS XVII is particularly striking, as the playback stops very suddenly, followed by a 4″ silence. While separating the playback and ensemble segments by silence may seem an obvious strategy to employ, this is in fact the first time in the entire work Xenakis does it.

ES XXI is very brief, 22″, and the next ensemble segment even briefer at just 10″. The first segment is a single block of woodwinds with the horns, playing glissandi in middle and low registers, the undulations complicated by fixed notes played staccato or flutter-tongue, or with rapid dynamic fluctuations. The phrases are otherwise distinguished by widely varying dynamics, from *pp* to *fff*.

At 58:38, PS XVIII takes over, but only briefly, confounding the expectation of another long stretch of playback. This segment again brusquely cuts off before the start of ES XXII, this time providing a window of silence of just 2″. In these two moments of silence between playback and ensemble segments, it is apparent how different the effect is for an ensemble to finish playing its material, even if stopping suddenly, and cutting a tape with material that is continuous. For Xenakis, the strategy is the same, and we have noted numerous instances in the score where a block of material is cut off then taken up again later, sometimes quite some time later, not necessarily in temporal succession. But, in the studio, when the tape is cut the amplitudes of the recorded material return instantly to zero, potentially creating artifacts (clicks) due to the limitations of audio equipment to convey such sudden shifts. The ensemble instruments continue to resonate slightly when cut off, while no such resonance occurs in the studio, unless added as an additional effect. These two moments of silence cut between the playback and ensemble segments draw even stronger attention to the differences between the two media.

ES XXII shifts to the strings alone, a quick outburst of the dense mixed material shifting to a sustained texture combining natural harmonics with detuned unisons. PS XIX starts right as the strings finish, and carries on for well over 8 minutes, by far the longest segment of the entire work. This segment contains longer stretches than elsewhere of more or less clear layers of brass (sustained or repeated-note textures) and high woodwinds.

At 60:00, ES XXIII starts up, the only time that the ensemble intervenes while the playback continues (there are three earlier occurrences of the opposite, where playback segments occur while the ensemble plays on). This segment, which includes both winds and strings, disrupts the listening strategy of the earlier lengthy playback segment, where the tension of always comparing the live and recorded material had been relaxed. The winds are present through the full 42″ of ES XXIII, playing repeated notes legato, in different rhythmic divisions to create cross-rhythmic pulsations. The composite harmony gradually evolves higher, and the articulation shifts to staccato to end, along with a ramping up of the dynamics to *ffff*. At 60:16 the strings launch a brief passage of the dense mixed texture that has appeared often throughout *Kraanerg*. PS XIX continues for several more minutes, and in fact continues for 42″ after the start of ES XXIV at 67:00.

The final ensemble segment is quite substantial at 2′06″. It continues until the final playback segment starts in at 69:06. Unusually, the strings and winds begin together here. The strings play the sustained texture of detuned unison double-stops last heard on its own in ES XVIII. The brass, joined by woodwinds, enter with the legato repeated notes taken up from ES XXIII. Starting with the trumpets, the density of this texture gradually fills out, and the dynamics ramp up from *mf* to *fff*. At 67:14 the woodwinds switch briefly to staccato articulations, and this change is followed by a new block in the strings, the by now very familiar active, mixed texture. The strings are cut off at 67:26, but the winds carry on the repeated notes until 67:34, when a new woodwind block takes over, a composite of short held notes, sometimes played staccato, flutter-tongue, or quilisma, with sharp accents and exaggerated dynamic profiles. The low woodwinds carry on throughout, while the higher instruments enter in four groups of staggered attacks. This block is cut at 67:58, reentering 4 seconds later, with the high woodwinds passing off to the lower instruments before being cut off again at 68:14.

The strings, meanwhile, come back in at 67:54, with the lower instruments playing sustained tones or double-stops, accented according to indicated rhythms, a familiar texture last heard in ES XX. The violins join the block at 68:12 just before the woodwinds are cut off. Accidentals in the string parts here are mostly third-tones, but the violas play quarter-tones, the only time in *Kraanerg* that these two tone divisions are combined. The strings are cut off at 68:24, picking up the same material again at 68:54. In an overlapping block, the brass enter at 68:18, sustaining upper-mid register notes elaborated by quilisma and dynamic fluctuations around *mf*. At 68:28 the brass shift to slowly unfurling glissando lines, sculpted with dynamic contours moving between *p* and *fff*. At 68:41 the brass land on held notes played *ffff*, switching to flutter-tongue then moving back to the glissandi. The brass finish up at 69:00, but the reentry of the accented sustained strings just before this carries through to 69:06, the end of the ensemble playing.

PS XX, the final segment of the work, starts up at 69:06, right where the ensemble finishes. This passage runs over 6 minutes, and continues with the interplay of the four layers of processed ensemble sounds, spatialized over the four channels of the sound system. The interplay between recognizable ensemble blocks and highly processed layers that was more prominent in PS XIX is again present here. Some of the textures that had become familiar from the ensemble segments—string harmonics, battuto, mixed string material including glissandi, winds repeated notes, quilisma passages—make their appearances. Toward the end, the playback material is subject to amplitude cuts in two of the channels, where the ongoing sounds are interrupted by rapid shifts to low/no volume, quickly returning to the levels from before. This modulation occurs at a rate slightly faster than once per second. While there had been amplitude cuts inserted into the primarily continuous flowing textures of the playback segments earlier, this is the only moment of regularly modulating studio technique imposed on the material. While unique in the work, it is not significant enough to constitute a closing gesture that would carry cadential import. The music just ends, the playback cut off; there is no fade out or climactic gesture.

Kraanerg ends as if in mid-stream. Given that there had been no such clear gestures in all of *Kraanerg* leading to that point, the lack of a traditionally understood sense of closure should not be surprising. The music functions differently, like a mosaic, or a kaleidoscope, the materials of the work being presented, shifting to other materials, returning, or returning with some parameter or other varied, the proportions fluctuating in a nonlinear manner. The way the music is put together implies that it could keep going, ever recombining its textures and entities. The significance of the lengthy playback segments that dominate Part Three does impart formal shape to the work on the global level, especially in comparison to Part One and Part Two, but the lack of significant changes in the sonic content of these segments from earlier ones weakens the sense of directionality on the moment-to-moment perceptual levels. One of the most fascinating aspects of *Kraanerg* is this sense of nondirectionality, while at the same time conveying a sense of continual renewal.

Annexes

The published score of *Kraanerg*, copied from the composer's manuscript, includes a page that Xenakis titles *Annexes*. It contains a number of musical gestures for the full strings and full winds, notated together (strings above the winds, unusually) but likely intended to be performed (recorded?) separately. The first event for the strings is a long glissando starting on a unison, with each instrument slowly sliding out to eventually land on a widespread chord. The resemblance to the opening of *Metastaseis* is striking, here scored for 12 rather than 46 strings. Xenakis gives a tempo marking of 20 à 240 MM, a dynamic marking of *pp ... ffff*, and an indication to move from normal bowing to ponticello. The second string gesture is an open indication to grind the strings by bowing with extreme pressure. There is no indication of duration. The third event is for cellos and basses, each playing their lowest string tuned an octave lower than normal, at a dynamic marking of *fff*, again with an open indication of duration. At that dynamic marking, the resulting sounds would be quite unstable, given how loose the detuned strings would be (Xenakis used this technique before, in *ST/4*, from 1962, and in *Nomos alpha*, from 1966).

The winds have two gestures notated. The first is a wide-register chord, notated as a single beat, marked *sfffpp*, with a one-beat preparatory crescendo of low notes. The pitches include quarter-tones. The second element is another wide-register chord, this time sustained at *fff*, with an indication of quilisma. There is an annotation asking that the instruments play separately, then by groups, etc.

What are these "annexes" intended for? The most likely conjecture is that Xenakis used them as material for the recorded elements produced in the studio. The grinding strings are found in various playback segments, as is the held quilisma sonority in the winds. It is possible that the detuned low strings were used to create the nebulous low drones that are often present in the playback segments, but the processing makes it difficult to confirm this. The sharply attacked winds chord is not obviously present in the finished playback segments, and the fanning-out string glissando may well be present, but it is nowhere obvious, apart from brief moments (where it may have been performed at the fastest indicated tempo).

In addition, it is worth noting that there is much else in the playback segments that could not have come from these annexes, the repeated note textures in the winds, for example, or the battuto textures of the strings. So, the question as to the purpose and import of these annex materials remains. There is no explanation given in the foreword to the score or anywhere else in the known archival materials, and there is no record of Xenakis discussing it, as he makes very little mention of *Kraanerg* in any publications beyond the notes for the premiere and the publicity around it. This page of extra music appended to the score is enigmatic, and fascinating.

Chapter 5
Reception

Lead-up

Kraanerg was premiered on 2 June 1969 at a gala performance to celebrate the opening of the National Arts Centre (NAC) in Ottawa. Canadian Prime Minister Pierre Elliott Trudeau and Governor General Roland Michener were in attendance, along with local, national, and international dignitaries. A large press corps was there to report on the occasion. The National Ballet of Canada dedicated two months to rehearse with Roland Petit on the choreography for the new work. The final week was spent in Ottawa in the new hall, as designer Victor Vasarely's set design was installed and the lighting coordinated. The company orchestra rehearsed with conductor Lukas Foss to master the difficult score and to synchronize the music with the audio technicians responsible for playback of the four-track tape segments and for diffusion and balance of the sounds in the hall on a sophisticated audio system never before used.

Composer Iannis Xenakis was also there, but his work had mostly been completed months earlier. As mentioned earlier, given the complexity of the score, and given the substantial role the electroacoustic element played in the composition, there was no other way to work on the choreography except to make a complete recording of the music to rehearse with. A rehearsal pianist would have been of no use in this case, as so much of the music could not be reduced to a keyboard score. This meant that, by March 1969, Xenakis needed to have completed the score, produced the electroacoustic component, ensured production of the orchestral parts for the musicians, and arranged to record the music. As noted earlier, Xenakis had a good working relationship with Marius Constant, who directed the Ensemble Ars Nova, resident at Radio France (ORTF) in Paris. In spite of his professorship in Indiana during that time, Xenakis and Constant were able to set up the rehearsals and recording sessions at Radio France. At the same time, Xenakis had booked time at Studio Acousti in Paris to produce the four-channel pre-recorded elements of *Kraanerg*. With all of this material, Xenakis arranged to mix it all down at the GRM studios at Radio France, where François Bayle was then Director.

Archival records at the National Ballet of Canada indicate that Xenakis sent the complete recording to the company in Toronto on 6 March 1969. Xenakis's publisher, Boosey & Hawkes, sent the full score and parts on 13 March 1969. A letter from Xenakis dated 17 April 1969 reports that he planned to bring a copy of the tape to Roland Petit on 27 April 1969 when he was to travel to Toronto (from Oberlin, Ohio, where he was giving lectures, on his way back to Bloomington). He seems to be referring to the performance materials (the four-track recordings that would include only the playback segments).

At that time, there was a great deal of discussion between Xenakis, Boosey & Hawkes, and the National Ballet of Canada about releasing a recording of *Kraanerg*, possibly in time for the premiere. The situation was very unusual, as, normally, the premiere would be the first time a composition is heard; a recording might follow on from there, or might follow from a radio recording of the premiere originally intended for broadcast. In the case of *Kraanerg*, a recording was already done, the quality obviously good enough that commercial release could be considered. As it turned out, Erato agreed to release the recording, but it was not ready for the premiere. It came out later in 1969, as part of a box set of five discs featuring Xenakis's music. *Kraanerg* took up two discs of the set: the other works included were: *Syrmos* for 18 strings, *Polytope de Montréal* for four ensembles, and *Medea* for male chorus and ensemble, all recorded by Ensemble Ars Nova and previously released by Erato as an individual LP. The fourth disc included Xenakis's two spatialized orchestral works: *Terretektorh* (1966) and *Nomos gamma* (1968), performed by the Orchestre Philharmonique de l'ORTF, conducted by Charles Bruch. The final disc of the set collected Xenakis's early electroacoustic works: *Bohor* (1962), *Diamorphoses* (1957), *Orient-Occident* (1960), and *Concret PH* (1958). This box set saw some critical success, but *Kraanerg* was little discussed in the press, perhaps because it had not yet been presented live in Europe.

Much of the advance publicity for the gala opening focused on the NAC itself. There was controversy around the architecture, and around the expense. As Ottawa journalist Greg Connolley reported, "It has been called a monstrosity and a national disgrace."[1] Another (uncredited) column in the same issue of the local newspaper mentions an earlier editorial headline, speaking to a commonly held view that this grand cultural project was elitist: "To an Ottawa aristocrat building you a culture palace, what's $46,000,000?" Also in the same issue, journalist Krista Maeots reports how:

> the public's views of the arts centre project have changed gradually, as it has evolved from a 'traffic obstruction' and 'hole in Confederation Park' to a 'fortress,' 'wheat elevator' and 'penitentiary', and finally to an 'iceberg' with marvels hidden beneath the surface.[2]

As architect Fred Lebensold observed to her: "The exterior is made of good Canadian natural materials and fits its surroundings ... Those who criticize it should get to know it by walking through ... experiencing it."[3]

On 31 May 1969, the Centre was opened to the public so they could indeed experience it in person. As Prime Minister Trudeau noted at the inauguration: "This

---

[1] Greg Connolley, "National Arts Centre: A cultural equivalent to Bonaventure ...?," *Ottawa Citizen* (30 May 1969), 56.
[2] Krista Maeots, "Completion was highlight,' *Ottawa Citizen* (30 May 1969), 58.
[3] Maeots 1969, 58.

is a wonderfully well-endowed instrument. It now needs only to be played." Outdoor and foyer performances of popular or folkloric music were presented that opening weekend, the aim being to create a friendly, festival-like atmosphere. The scene was set for the unveiling of the interior performances spaces on Monday, 2 June.

The main stage was to be inaugurated by the National Ballet of Canada, and this was the highpoint of the gala celebrations. The smaller stages presented Canadian theater works, representing both English and French activities, mainly centered in Toronto and Montreal (Ottawa, as the country's capital, is officially bilingual and supports both traditions in all its cultural activities). Quebec author and playwright Michel Tremblay collaborated with director André Brassard on a modern, topical adaptation of a classical Greek play, *Lysistrata, d'après Aristophanes*. From Toronto, playwright Jack Winter presented his new work, *Party Day*. Finally, *Orphée*, a new chamber opera by Montreal composer and television producer Gabriel Charpentier, was premiered.

In spite of ample Canadian content for the opening of the NAC, there had been some controversy that such a major commission as a new full-length ballet would be awarded to a French choreographer and a Greek-French composer. As Canadian composer Norma Beecroft noted:

> the 1960s was a time when Canadian composers were only just beginning to gain recognition, having very few opportunities to have their music performed. The only organization for contemporary music in the country was the Société de Musique Contemporaine du Québec, founded in 1966.[4]

Lauretta Thistle, writing in *The Canadian Composer* newsletter, was more pointed:

> What possible explanation can there be for going outside Canada for such important assignments? The answer is that the National Ballet has been accustomed to going outside Canada for its prestige works ... The matter would not be as serious if Mr. Petit's reputation were more secure. He is newsworthy but hardly trustworthy ... Another time, it would be an honour to have a Xenakis ballet. But for the opening of the NAC, having him and passing over Canadian composers is greatly to be deplored.[5]

As an answer to these criticisms, the National Ballet added a curtain raiser to the gala program. *The Queen/La Reine* was a short, patriotic work choreographed by National Ballet resident Grant Strate to music by Louis Applebaum, a Canadian composer especially known for his film scores. While this gesture may have

---

[4] Norma Beecroft, "Xenakis à Toronto: Vision personelle," in *Regards sur Iannis Xenakis*, Hugues Gerhards, editor (Paris: Stock, 1981, 316, my translation).
[5] Lauretta Thistle, "National Arts Centre gala," *The Canadian Composer* (February 1969).

assuaged some, it did nothing for others. Ralph Hicklin, reporting for a Toronto newspaper, saw through the apparent ruse: "Having had the courage to commission an international ballet, the National Ballet should not have backwatered, and offered this sop to the critics who have been yapping for an all-Canadian ballet to open the National Arts Centre … It will probably never be seen again."[6] Influential New York dance critic Clive Barnes paid much attention to the gala event in Ottawa, but was equally dismissive of the Strate/Applebaum opener: "Nothing *rien* need be said."[7]

The Gala

Going into the premiere of *Kraanerg*, the advance publicity included a statement from the composer: "The ballet has no symbolism but is a dialogue on the ideological disorders that will face the world when mushrooming birthrates mean 70 or 80 per cent of the population is younger than 30."[8] As noted earlier, the years 1968 and 1969 saw numerous examples of these "ideological disorders," a situation of which Xenakis, having been almost killed as a young man for the convictions of his beliefs, was acutely aware. Social upheaval was very much current at that time (protests, social reform, civil rights, cultural rebellion). In other developments, technology was evolving rapidly: the first lunar landing took place right around the same time as *Kraanerg*, in July 1969; Stanley Kubrick's film, *2001: A Space Odyssey*, popularizing not only issues of space travel but also computers and artificial intelligence, was released in 1968. The modernist score for *Kraanerg*, the addition of a technological element to the music, the striking op-art stage design, all underscored a forward-looking aesthetic stance that was also highlighted by the architecture of the NAC itself.

In the program booklet, the synopsis presented by Petit is terse:

> Iannis Xenakis created the title *Kraanerg* by placing two ancient Greek words together, 'Kraan' means to perfect, to accomplish; 'erg' signifies energy.
>
> *Kraanerg* has no plot. Each of us must freely interpret the choreography. The movement is sometimes horizontal (the dancers seemingly floating in space), sometimes primitive, even athletic.
>
> *Kraanerg*'s atmospheric environment is established by Victor Vasarely's black and white decors. In ancient times the circle symbolized earthly paradise and

---

[6] Ralph Hicklin, "National Arts Centre debut: Ballet beats first-night novelty," *The Telegram* (3 June 1969).

[7] Clive Barnes, "Dance: Ballet by Xenakis opens Ottawa Arts Center," *New York Times* (4 June 1969).

[8] Iannis Xenakis, "Press release" (Ottawa: National Arts Centre, May 1969).

the square, celestial paradise. However, in topology, these two symbols have the same significance.

> I have created my ballet with the complicity of the dancers. We have tried to use all our energy to attain a sense of accomplishment and perhaps, with a little luck, each of us will approach his own level of perfection.[9]

In terms of the dancing itself, the company had never before worked with music like *Kraanerg*. As Veronica Tennant, then a principal dancer with the National Ballet of Canada, recounts:

> But the first time we heard the music, [the reaction] was, 'how can one dance to a score like this?' It's intriguing, it's stunning, it's shocking, it's frightening at times, but how does one dance to it? Well, Roland Petit devised something very radical, I think, in that we didn't follow the music at all. And this was difficult for someone like me, who loves to be pushed by the music, and to respond to the music. But what we had to do in this particular instance … is to have our own rhythm. So … Daniel Sellier, … our ballet master, would stand in the front wing, and he had a little microphone with him and he would tap the … rhythms that were devised for us … For the entire ballet, he was our metronome, or our prompter, so that we could be dancing in unison, or even separately. He was *our* conductor. And it was just the most extraordinary experience.[10]

This method of dance production is common with choreographers such as Merce Cunningham, working with music that very often is conceived completely independently of the dance; but Cunningham worked with his own dancers, not those of other companies. An approach to learning an extended dance work without relying on the music would have been very unusual for a classically based company such as the National Ballet of Canada.

So, the stage was set, the curtain was raised. In the end, there are no reports of a huge standing ovation by the audience (nonetheless, one account mentions 10 minutes of clapping and cheering), but most accounts grant that *Kraanerg* was a major accomplishment. An editorial the next day in a local newspaper acknowledged the value not only of the work but also of the role of the NAC:

> Art … is not an end in itself but a means of addressing humanity. The object of the Arts Centre is to help Canadians address and hear humanity … The pursuit of art, the embracing of art in our personal and national life must be not just a pursuit of the familiar, it must puzzle us, annoy us, amuse us, broaden us, humble us, inspire us, so that we can become accustomed to the idea … that something

---

[9] Petit 1969b.
[10] Veronica Tennant, "Interview: On *Kraanerg*," Mode Records DVD 196 (2008).

we don't at once understand may be worth understanding ... Years and years ago [Alphonse] Daudet wrote that 'music is another planet', and some ears found this music even more unfamiliar than the astronauts have found the moon. And yet, and yet ... the ballet told the eyes it was something to do with man's urge to attain perfection and once one ceased seeking a 'plot' there was artistry enough to sooth the savage ears.[11]

Toronto critic Herbert Whittaker also underscored the importance of the opening of the NAC with such a modern creation:

The work, *Kraanerg*, which, without ever dropping to symbolism, much less more representative forms, advances a dark forbidding vision of a world conflict of new sinister forces ... Always the stage was fascinatingly filled with energetic movement, though it was not always meaningful ... but the end of first night ... left only one thing clear about the future: we have achieved this great new central focus to Canada's theatrical culture; there is no retreat.[12]

Veronica Tennant recalls how the show felt from the stage:

I think the audience was totally shocked ... It was pretty quiet out there. I don't quite know what they knew to make of this wave of originality ... We were really pushing every side of more than an envelope. In this case, it was just every boundary that you could think of—in the music, in the choreography, in the design, and in the whole envelopment of space and projection of unusual artistic drama in space ... When you're ... brave and provocative in art and you combine the art forms you really push people who don't necessarily want to be pushed in directions that they don't necessarily want to go, and it's often in retrospect where people go 'My goodness that was spectacular!' At the time, they are uncertain.[13]

The Critics

Other newspaper reports make more of a distinction between the different elements of the *Kraanerg* performance premiere. Montreal reporter Zelda Heller writes:

It would not be entirely fair to call it Roland Petit's ballet ... because the work's aim is so obviously total spectacle, with the other elements—Iannis Xenakis's music

---

[11] Editorial, "The National Arts Centre—Like 'Another Planet,'" *Ottawa Journal* (3 June 1969).
[12] Herbert Whittaker, "Petit's Kraanerg discloses dark vision of cosmic chaos," *Globe and Mail* (4 June 1969).
[13] Tennant 2008.

and Vasarely and Yvaral's decor—carrying equal weight with the dance in the total effect ... The Xenakis score is munificent, romantic, contemporary, sonorous magnificence ... Here's music that's passionate, directly physical in its impact, while remaining within the stark stochastic idiom the composer has carved for himself ... For the occasion Petit, too, has tried to abandon himself to sincerity ... But frequently these scenes succeeded each other in a loose kaleidoscopic way, strong in their own elements but weak or stiff in their connective tissue. Perhaps the chief reproach ... would be that he has not dared to go far enough into his own thought. Sometimes he abandons his own ideas ... and he then opts for the kind of superficial facilities that characterized some of his earlier work.[14]

In the words of French critic Maurice Fleuret:

Energetic and accomplished, the music of Xenakis is a great abstract poem, of astral resonances ... It is a work of accomplishment, of radiant maturity ... In the face of this superhuman sonic universe, under Vasarely's huge suspended globes and cubes, in front of the fascinating optical illusions, Roland Petit necessarily seemed to be crushed. A man of familiar gesture and anecdote ... abstraction and symbol are not his *forte*.[15]

New York critic Clive Barnes was even more pointed in his praise for the music and reservations for the choreography:

It is a wonderful piece of music, enthralling, and one that grips the mind and the heart. Indeed, even at a single hearing, I would feel inclined to say that it is one of the major ballet scores of the century. The choreography by Roland Petit is totally inadequate to the music. Mr. Xenakis's music, with its gushes and rushes of sound, its architectural build-ups into aural space, its strange and chilling sonorities, its curious interplay between taped sound and orchestral musicians, is wonderfully exciting ... Mr. Petit is rather an old-fashioned choreographer ... His ideas of modernism are trivial—it looks like a mixture of Serge Lifar classicism and Maurice Béjart calisthenics. The groupings are often formal, the invention is both pained and painful, and his sensibility toward the music appears minimal.[16]

By the time the National Ballet presented *Kraanerg* to European audiences in 1972, it seems the die was cast. The comments by London critic James Kennedy are representative: "'*Kraanerg*' shows what [these dancers] can do if they must. It is a

---

[14] Zelda Heller, "National Arts Centre: National Ballet of Canada," *Montreal Star* (3 June 1969), 34–5.

[15] Maurice Fleuret, "Création de *Kraanerg* de Xenakis, R. Petit et Vasarely au Centre national des Arts d'Ottawa," *Nouvel Observateur* (17 June 1969), my translation.

[16] Barnes 1969.

two-act work and, it must be said, a rather dreadful one—long-drawn, pretentious, and unstylish."[17] The critics praised the dancers, the design, sometimes the music, but very rarely the choreography.

In spite of the best efforts of the National Ballet of Canada to perform and tour the work, *Kraanerg* was not a successful dance piece. After 1972, it disappeared into storage and into the archives. Nonetheless, it was an extraordinarily ambitious and courageous project for the company and for all concerned.

---

[17] James Kennedy, "Canadian Ballet," *The Guardian* (22 May 1972).

Chapter 6
Performance History

National Ballet of Canada

The National Ballet of Canada performed *Kraanerg* twice during its run in Ottawa at the National Arts Centre in June 1969. These shows on 2 June and 4 June were interspersed with presentations of two ballets already in the company's repertoire: Prokofiev's *Romeo and Juliet* (choreographed by John Cranko, for Stuttgart Ballet) featuring Edward Villella from New York City Ballet (who did not dance in *Kraanerg* even though he is listed in the program); and Tchaikovsky's *Swan Lake* (choreographed by Erik Bruhn, for the National Ballet of Canada). The new work was presented to the home audience in Toronto the following season.

The agreement between the National Ballet of Canada and Boosey & Hawkes gave exclusive performance rights for *Kraanerg* to the company for two years, through 31 August 1971, for performances in Canada, the USA, and Europe. This agreement was later extended for another year, to cover a planned European tour in the spring of 1972. In return, the National Ballet committed to 50 performances of the work (or to pay the contracted royalties for this number of presentations).

As it turned out, the company fell well short of the targeted number of performances. After the premiere performances in Ottawa, *Kraanerg* was programmed for a run of six shows in Toronto in November 1969 (see Table 6.1). The following season the National Ballet took the work on its West Coast tour in January–February 1971 and included a couple more Toronto performances later that spring. The following season, *Kraanerg* was presented in Europe during the company's tour in May–June 1972.

And there it ended. The expense of touring *Kraanerg*, with the additional musicians, instruments, audio equipment, technicians, and large set design, would surely have been challenging to carry for long. In addition, the provocative intensity of the music would have made it difficult to integrate the work into the company's long-term repertoire at home in Toronto (in contrast to, say, *The Nutcracker*, a work the National Ballet of Canada presents every year). It was no doubt more economical for the company to pay off the outstanding royalties to Boosey & Hawkes than to continue to perform the work.

Beyond the Premiere Run

Dance companies who commission new productions quite naturally hope for other companies to take the work up, helping to recover costs and enhancing their reputations as innovative organizations. Sadly, Roland Petit's choreography for

Table 6.1   List of performances of *Kraanerg* by the National Ballet of Canada

Performance	Date	Venue/Location
1	2 June 1969	National Arts Centre, Ottawa
2	4 June 1969	National Arts Centre, Ottawa
3	18 November 1969	Toronto
4	19 November 1969	Toronto
5	20 November 1969	Toronto
6	21 November 1969	Toronto
7	22 November 1969 (matinee)	Toronto
8	22 November 1969	Toronto
9	21 January 1971	San Diego
10	22 January 1971	Los Angeles
11	27 January 1971	Berkeley
12	28 January 1971	Berkeley
13	3 February 1971	Vancouver
14	22 April 1971	Toronto
15	29 April 1971	Toronto
16	20 May 1972	Coliseum, London
17	22 May 1972	Coliseum, London
18	17 June 1972	Théâtre Royal de la Monnaie, Brussels
19	23 June 1972	King's Theatre, Glasgow

Kraanerg was never taken up by any other company. Further, according to National Ballet of Canada historian James Neufeld, Petit himself realized the production was dated, reporting that the choreographer requested that the company *not* present *Kraanerg* in Paris during its 1972 European tour.[1] The less-than-enthusiastic critical reception of his work no doubt contributed to this circumstance as well. The difficulties of Xenakis's score along with the logistical issues of integrating the four-channel recorded elements would likely have also contributed to the work's lack of appeal to other dance companies. With the notable exception of the Merce Cunningham Dance Company and a few others, most dance groups do not easily incorporate cutting-edge music performance into their ongoing practice. Understandably, resources are usually focused on cutting-edge choreography. In the case of *Kraanerg*, the most innovative elements of the work were the music and the design rather than the choreography. This made it rather a strange fit for the dance community.

---

[1] James Neufeld, *Passion to Dance: The National Ballet of Canada* (Toronto: Dundurn, 2011), 149–50.

The call by critic Clive Barnes to bring the work (the music and design) to New York with a new choreography by George Balanchine went unheeded. In fact, it would take until 1988 for *Kraanerg* to make a new appearance on the dance stage. In the meantime, at least the music was known from the Erato recording that was released in 1969. While the five-box set of Xenakis's music may not have been a bestseller (it went out of print fairly quickly, and was never re-issued on CD), it was nonetheless awarded the Grand Prix du Disque from the Académie du Disque Français in 1970, and the Japanese release was awarded the Nippon Music Award in 1971.

Xenakis himself rarely mentioned *Kraanerg*, either in print or in interview. Biographer Nouritza Matossian does not discuss it at all, even though she covers his life right through this period. Interviewer Bálint András Varga asked the composer about the piece, but Xenakis only admitted that the pre-recorded part was produced under difficult circumstances and that he should do another.[2] Within the context of a discussion with Varga about his electroacoustic music, Xenakis may have been thinking of how he re-did the material for *Concret PH*, given that the original was produced in 1958 under severe time constraints and in a facility lacking the technology he was used to at GRM. But, otherwise, of the largest work Xenakis had ever written, he says nothing else, and Varga does not seem to be interested in pursuing the discussion. As the composer's wife, Françoise Xenakis, recounts:

> I think that [with regard to *Kraanerg*] he had to remove himself from it. He did not discuss it after the first performance ... When he was not satisfied, he withdrew into his shell. I think he had believed in it, and it didn't turn out to be a success.[3]

It may well have been Xenakis's own reaction to the *spectacle* of the premiere that led, in 1977, to an intervention that resulted in the re-issue on vinyl of the Erato box set, but with *Oresteïa* (which had been issued separately) substituting for *Kraanerg*.

Concert Performances

In spite of the National Ballet of Canada having exclusive rights to *Kraanerg* through 1971, then 1972, Marius Constant and Ensemble Ars Nova mounted an exceptional concert performance of the work in Paris in 1971 (see Table 6.2). Of course, Constant and his ensemble had recorded *Kraanerg* in 1969, so they would no doubt have been able to give a convincing presentation of it. While there is note of this concert in the press, it is unlikely Xenakis was present (at that time, he was still a

---

[2] Varga 1996, 110.
[3] Françoise Xenakis, "Interview: On *Kraanerg*," Mode Records DVD 196.

Table 6.2 List of concert performances of *Kraanerg*

Date	Location	Performers
1 April 1971	Paris	Ensemble Ars Nova, Marius Constant
12 December 1977	Paris	Ensemble 2e2m, Paul Méfano
28 April 1995	London	Reservoir, Mikel Toms
12 November 1996	New York	ST-X Ensemble, Charles Zachary Bornstein
19 November 1996	Princeton	ST-X Ensemble, Charles Zachary Bornstein
7 March 2006	Boston	Callithumpian Consort, Stephen Drury
25 April 2007	Vienna	Klangforum Wien, Peter Rundel
4 October 2007	Venice	Klangforum Wien, Stefan Asbury
3 April 2009	Vancouver	Vancouver New Music, Giorgio Magnanensi
5 June 2011	Amsterdam	Holland Festival, Visual Kitchen (light show), Asko|Schönberg Ensemble, Arturo Tamayo
13 July 2011	Reims	Les Flâneries Musicales de Reims, Asko|Schönberg Ensemble, Arturo Tamayo

professor at Indiana University), and the attention the concert received was minimal. It seems to have done nothing to reform *Kraanerg*'s reputation.

After the concert performance in Paris in April 1971, and the four European performances by the National Ballet of Canada in 1972, *Kraanerg* disappeared from the stage for five years. Then, in late 1977, French journalist and administrator Claude Samuel organized *Cycle Xenakis*, a major festival of Xenakis's music. A number of his orchestral works were performed, including the Paris premiere of *Antikhthon*, the score Xenakis wrote for Balanchine in 1971 to a commission for a new ballet that was never realized. On 12 December 1977, as part of this festival, Paul Méfano, a French composer-conductor a generation younger than Constant, presented *Kraanerg* in concert, with his Ensemble 2e2m, founded in 1972. There was more critical attention paid to the orchestral concerts of this festival (held in major central venues), especially the world premiere of a major new work, *Jonchaies*, which closed the festival on 21 December 1977. Nonetheless, it is significant that *Kraanerg* was included in this retrospective celebration of Xenakis's music.[4]

---

[4] Another factor in the slim performance history of *Kraanerg* may have been due to Xenakis's decision to change publishers from Boosey & Hawkes to Éditions Salabert beginning not long after the completion of *Kraanerg*. While Salabert listed this and earlier works in the catalogue, it would likely not have done much to promote works for which it lacked the publishing rights. And, for its part, Boosey & Hawkes no longer carried an investment in the lifelong activities of this composer, so may have scaled back its promotional efforts, especially for a work requiring such complicated and unusual resources to perform.

Sydney

In spite of this spotlight in Paris in 1977, *Kraanerg* subsequently sat on the shelf for over a decade. In the meantime, Xenakis made the acquaintance of a talented pianist from Australia, Roger Woodward (b. 1942). *Mists*, for solo piano, was written for him in 1980, and *Keqrops*, for piano and orchestra, in 1986. Through the long process of learning the concerto, then of working through the rehearsals and performances with the New York Philharmonic (conducted by Zubin Mehta) in the presence of the composer, Woodward became very much immersed in the music of Xenakis.[5] In the aftermath of this overwhelming experience, Woodward hit upon an audacious idea: to mount a new staging of *Kraanerg*!

To do this, he needed to find a willing choreographer, and a willing dance company. In the first, by good fortune, Woodward found the second. Graeme Murphy (b. 1950), Australian choreographer, by 1988 had been Artistic Director of the Sydney Dance Company since 1976 and was a major figure in Australian dance and beyond. In agreeing to take *Kraanerg* on, Murphy brought it to his company, not only to dance it, but also to present it as the finale of the 1988 season. That year was very important in Australia—it was the nation's bicentennial. With all the celebrations, both cultural and social, Murphy chose to make *Kraanerg* the climactic highlight of that significant season. Like the National Ballet of Canada and the National Arts Centre in Ottawa, the Sydney Dance Company, resident at the Sydney Opera House (in itself an iconic creation, designed by Danish architect Jørn Utzon, first opened in 1973), wanted to spotlight its confident place in the international *milieu*. Any nationalistic grumblings about giving such prominence to the work of a non-Australian composer were offset by the fact that everyone else involved—the choreographer, dancers, designer, conductor, musicians—were all local artists. Woodward put together a crack group of new music specialists for the project, and named it the Alpha Centauri Ensemble, after the brightest star of the southern skies. Murphy brought in George Freedman, a well-known architect and interior designer, to do the design, along with Jennifer Irwin for costumes and John Drummond Montgomery for lighting. The set consisted of a tower framework in white that set off colours and shadows from the lighting design, with the dancers wearing unisex costumes of bright colours.

Murphy's approach to the choreography was to work in parallel to the music, to create an ever-changing continuous flow of dance movement (without intermission) that would sustain the same intensity of energy as the score. The critics by and large found the work fascinating and powerful. According to William Shoubridge, writing after the premiere:

---

[5] Roger Woodward, "Conquering Goliath: Preparing and performing Xenakis' *Keqrops*," in *Performing Xenakis*, Sharon Kanach, editor (Hillsdale, NY: Pendragon, 2010), 129–55.

Figure 6.1   Image from Graeme Murphy's choreography of *Kraanerg*, featuring dancers Jan Pinkerton and Stefan Karlsson (photographer, Branco Gaica)

> *Kraanerg* has no plot, narrative or sentiment and no balletic expositions for the eye to hang on to. It has more in common with the rules of engineering or the concussions and collisions of molecules in space than with the *plastique* of body parts, yet it is as viscerally exciting to the eye as the music is challenging to the ear. … They [the dancers] all rise to the occasion and fill the stage space with a focused energy so intense that it leaves the audience shell-shocked and woozy.[6]

Critic Brian Hoad was aware of the original choreography by Petit, and was able to draw some comparison:

> How do you choreograph this apocalyptic music? The simple answer is, you can't. Petit tried in 1969 and was overwhelmed … Instead, having absorbed the music, Murphy came to regard it as a great building, some gigantic powerhouse which had to be entered with dance of complementary energy—dance which he then created in silence … There are moments when the music threatens to overwhelm the dancers completely but, instead, serves to drive them on with ever greater speed and intensity into new, virile forms of expression in pure dance. As an evening of dance, it is outstanding. As an evening of music, it is outstanding. But, performed in parallel, the dance inspired by the music yet totally different, the two streams

---

[6] William Shoubridge, "Dance: Murphy scores a thrilling success," *The Australian* (7 November 1988).

touching yet never merging, it all becomes an astonishing display of the creative process at work.[7]

Between 4 and 26 November, *Kraanerg* ran for 23 performances, more than the National Ballet of Canada presented in three years. This accomplishment in itself would have been extraordinarily intense for dancers and musicians, and is impressive for bringing out daily audiences of good numbers to the Sydney Opera House for this modernist, experimental production. At the same time, Woodward organized a recording session on 24 November 1988, to take advantage of the keenly honed focus and experience of the musicians. The resulting disc, released early in 1989, was the first new recording of *Kraanerg* since the original release in 1969, and the first to be put out as a compact disc (see Table 6.3 for the list of recordings). While there were plans to tour *Kraanerg* to Europe, nothing materialized, and Murphy never reprised the work in subsequent seasons, so the CD remains the sole document of this amazing, audacious project.

Table 6.3   Commercial recordings of *Kraanerg*

Year	Performers	Label
1969	Ensemble Ars Nova, Marius Constant	Erato STU 70527/28
1989	Alpha Centauri Ensemble, Roger Woodward	Etcetera KTC 1075
1997	ST-X Ensemble, Charles Zachary Bornstein	Asphodel 0975
2003	Sinfonieorchester Basel, Alexander Winterson	Col Legno WWE 1CDS 20217
2008	Callithumpian Consort, Stephen Drury	Mode 196 DVD/CD

In spite of the new choreography from Sydney not receiving any exposure in Europe, the recording, which received a good deal of critical attention, served to draw more interest to *Kraanerg*. This work, now with an acclaimed production behind it, and the new recording, started to be reconsidered as a major opus in Xenakis's *oeuvre* rather than an ignored one. Performances and productions started to occur more often.

Europe and North America

Swiss choreographer Pierre Wyss, working in Germany at the Staatstheater Wiesbaden, presented a new work in October 1991, *Lulu-Szenen*, using excerpts of scores by Xenakis. He followed this in February 1992 with *Oedipus, der Mensch*, which again used excerpts by Xenakis (and John Cage), this time including

---

[7] Brian Hoad, "Murphy's new journey," *The Bulletin* (22 November 1988), 125.

Kraanerg. The first European production of a new choreography of the complete *Kraanerg* took place in Germany in 1995, at the Deutsches Nationaltheater Weimar. Choreographer Joachim Schlömer worked closely with designer Frank Leimbach to create a work that portrayed the "struggle for accomplishment" of the title in a more narrative way than either Petit or Murphy. The dancers appear to grapple with winter, often dressed in overcoats, sometimes pulling sleds, snowflakes occasionally falling. Water is another primal element that is suggested in both the dance and the design. The movements are often slow, as if almost frozen, or weighed down in snow or water.

The run of *Kraanerg* in Weimar in March 1995 was a critical success, and the production was reprised in January–February 1999 for several performances in Basel, Switzerland. The musicians were this time drawn from the Sinfonieorchester Basel, under the direction of British conductor Alexander Winterson. A recording of *Kraanerg* with these musicians was produced in 2001 and released on the Col Legno label in 2003.

In the meantime, the first London performance of *Kraanerg* since the National Ballet of Canada's residency at the Coliseum in May 1972 took place in April 1995, this time as a concert performance. Reservoir, an ensemble specializing in contemporary music, presented the work at Conway Hall in the presence of the composer, and the event received some acclaim. As a follow-up, Xenakis was featured in an article-interview in *The Wire*, a UK-based music publication with an eclectic focus and wide readership (others featured in that issue include MC5, Sun Ra, Laurie Anderson, and The Future Sound of London). Author Ben Watson has been widely quoted for his description of the composer: "Xenakis has developed a music of truly majestic otherness. It is an alien shard, glimmering in the heart of the West."[8]

In New York, American conductor Charles Zachary Bornstein came under the spell of Xenakis's music and formed the ST-X Ensemble in 1994 for the sole purpose of performing and recording Xenakis's music. Over the next few years, Bornstein released five CDs of Xenakis's music, and gave several performances, in New York and elsewhere. One of his most ambitious projects was a concert presentation of *Kraanerg*, which was done both in New York and in Princeton in November 1996. To ramp up the publicity for the shows, Bornstein brought in DJ Spooky, a popular figure in the turntable/techno world, to run sound and trigger the playback segments. Spooky (Paul Miller) is a highly articulate artist and writer, and was already an admirer of Xenakis's work. The concerts attracted lots of attention, and the subsequent recording of *Kraanerg* by the ST-X Ensemble was released on the Asphodel label, known primarily for its electronica artists.

This American release of *Kraanerg* in 1997 was the second CD recording of the work, followed by the Col Legno disc in 2003. Clearly, this composition was gaining a strong presence as a concert work and as something to listen to

---

[8] Ben Watson, "Primal architect," *The Wire* 136 (June 1995), 20–24.

without the addition of dancers and stage production. At long last, 30 or so years after its premiere, *Kraanerg* was starting to be considered an important number in Xenakis's opus. The same year as the Asphodel release, an article on *Kraanerg* appeared in *Musicworks*, a Canadian-based music publication.[9] This was the first study to examine the work in detail. Another followed in 2003 by noted researcher-journalist Rudolf Frisius, who also wrote an essay for the 2003 Col Legno release.[10]

In January 2004, an innovative new production of *Kraanerg* was presented in Berlin. Directed by video artist Daniel Kötter, this show combined multi-screen projections of dancers (and other elements) around the performance space. The filmed choreography was created by Sasha Waltz, and the Kammerensemble Neue Musik Berlin (performing live) was conducted by Roland Kluttig. In addition to the four-channel sound that surrounds the audience, the video projections surrounded the space, filling the entire front and side walls of the performance space (the Labor für Musik:theater). By the time of this production, the audio playback materials, hitherto only available on four-track analog tape, had been digitized, and sound engineer/artist Daniel Teige had done a careful restoration of the audio files, cleaning up the tape hiss, etc. The ability to use new digital technology to create a work that inhabits the space of the performance venue in images, lighting, and sound would no doubt have greatly appealed to the composer. Sadly, Xenakis did not live to experience this new generation of performance art, having passed away in 2001. Nonetheless, it is worth noting that his own work in multimedia "polytopes" greatly contributed to the development of new ways of using technology to produce original shows of light and sound integrated within specific architectural spaces.[11]

Kötter presented four performances of *Kraanerg* in Berlin in January 2004. This production has not traveled, even though it is more portable than earlier productions involving live dancers. Still, this innovative presentation has opened the way for hybrid performances that incorporate multimedia while not involving dance. In April 2009, Vancouver New Music presented the first Canadian performance of *Kraanerg* since the National Ballet of Canada's last Toronto dance performances of it in 1971. Composer-conductor Giorgio Magnanensi added a video presentation to the music, the images being abstracted from footage of the 1968 riots in Paris. Magnanensi was well aware that Xenakis had had these (and other) social upheavals very much in mind while composing *Kraanerg*. For the Dutch premiere at the Holland Festival in June 2011, an interactive, immersive light show was designed by Visual Kitchen of Brussels to go with the music. The

---

[9] James Harley and Maria Anna Harley, "Triumphs of modernity: Xenakis's *Kraanerg* at the National Arts Centre," *Musicworks* 76 (1997), 24–31.

[10] Rudolf Frisius, "Musical et extramusical chez Xenakis. A propos de *Kraanerg* et de *Nekuïa*," in *Iannis Xenakis, Gérard Grisey: La métaphore lumineuse*, Makis Solomos, editor (Paris: L'Harmattan, 2003), 193–212.

[11] Kanach 2008, 198–277.

performance took place within the striking architecture of Muziekgebouw, created in 2005 by the Danish architectural collective, 3XN.

Kraanerg is a difficult work to program. Even though digital technology eases the technical issues (i.e., triggering soundfiles on a computer rather than operating a tape machine with precise start-stop cues), the score is difficult to perform, involves a large, non-standard ensemble, and is a lengthy work to fit into a concert program. At 75 minutes in duration, *Kraanerg* is best presented on its own, but this is a long stretch of music to listen to without a break. Adding video or lighting components helps to keep the audience engaged, certainly. Incorporating dancers into the presentation is beyond the reach of most music ensembles or producers, and, as we have seen, there have been few dance companies interested in taking *Kraanerg* on. Given all that, it is significant that important ensembles have undertaken to perform the work. The Asko|Schönberg Ensemble, the foremost new music group in the Netherlands (formed in 2008 through the merger of two long-established groups, Asko and Schönberg), not only performed *Kraanerg* in Amsterdam but went on to perform it in France as well. These performances were conducted by Xenakis champion Arturo Tamayo, who led a series of recordings of Xenakis's orchestral music on Timpani Records with the Orchestre Philharmonique du Luxembourg, a project that did *not* include *Kraanerg*.[12] Klangforum Wien is another long-established and important new music group in Europe, and it presented *Kraanerg* both in Vienna and Venice in 2007.

The other significant performance to mention took place in Boston in March 2006. The Callithumpian Consort, led by conductor-pianist Stephen Drury, is an ensemble of professionals and advanced students based out of the New England Conservatory of Music. The public performance was followed by a recording session the next day, for Mode Records. This disc, released in 2008, was put out on both CD and DVD. The latter includes a surround-sound mix, the first recording to present *Kraanerg* with the four-channel playback material surrounding the listener as originally intended. As home theater systems have become more and more common, the DVD presentation of *Kraanerg* is a powerful medium for experiencing the music close to the way it was originally conceived. For this recording, producer Brian Brandt included video footage of the musicians performing the work, as well as creative footage that is intercut together with the playback segments of the music to help distinguish these from the live-recorded ensemble segments.

Success

Altogether, *Kraanerg* has been performed something like 65 times to date. It is unlikely that many of Xenakis's other large-scale works have received this number of presentations. Any composer would be pleased with such a performance record.

---

[12] The five discs of the series were released as a box set in 2011 (Timpani 5C1177).

In this case, though, the initial negative critical reaction to the original choreography seems to have jinxed the piece, for presenters as well as the composer himself, at least initially. Thankfully, the expressive power of the music has outweighed the resistance to the work, and *Kraanerg* has rightfully gained its place as one of Xenakis's most important works, and as a landmark of contemporary music.

Chapter 7
Epilogue

For Xenakis, the experience of composing *Kraanerg* and then finding that the original choreography did not live up to his, or most critics', expectations was not a happy one. As the composer's wife Françoise has reflected, he withdrew from the work and put it aside. The powerful expression of his score would ultimately live on, though, through other choreographic productions, concert and multimedia presentations, and recordings. The composer himself, however, moved on. He only accepted one further commission for a dance work, that being *Antikhthon* for George Balanchine and his New York City Ballet, not long after the premiere of *Kraanerg*.

Xenakis never accepted another dance commission, although existing works of his continue to be set by various choreographers. He stayed away from the stage, too, for the most part. The only exception was his incidental music for a production of *The Bacchae*, Euripides' classical tragedy, for a 1993 production by the Opera Factory in London (directed by David Freeman). In addition, as noted earlier, Xenakis did compose additional pieces in 1987 and 1992 for his *Oresteïa* suite (originally composed in 1966). But, even though this music has been presented in staged productions on a number of occasions, the music was always intended to function in concert (the suite being put together from his original incidental music, which was never performed again after the 1966 performances in Ypsilanti, Michigan). *The Bacchae* was truly music for the theater, and has rarely been presented in concert (there is no recording to date).[1]

Robots

One dance project that did take up a good deal of the composer's attention in the late 1980s was a ballet for robots. German film director and composer Henning Lohner first met Xenakis in 1985 as a student. In 1986 Lohner published an interview with him,[2] and in 1987 began discussing the idea of a work involving robots. According to documents in the Xenakis Archives, the composer's first signed sketches relating to this project date from April 1988. It appears Xenakis was fascinated by the possibility of programming bodily movement. He had already created multimedia works ("polytopes") involving sound diffusion, flash bulbs, lasers, and moveable mirrors, where movement was conveyed both in sound and

---

[1] For a review of the original 1993 production of *The Bacchae* in London, see Malcolm Miller, "Xenakis's 'The Bacchae,'" *Tempo* 187 (December 1993), 36–7.

[2] Henning Lohner, "Interview with Iannis Xenakis." *Computer Music Journal* 10 (4), 1986, 50–55.

in light. Programming bodily movements would have been a natural extension of this activity. The field of robotics was in the early stages of its development in the 1980s, but there were already industrial applications, such as robotic equipment for assembly-line factories. Xenakis's sketches propose robots with humanoid limbs (arms, legs, head), with defined fields of movement that he could control by means of computer programming.

In his sketches, he wrote notes about the music (to be created on his UPIC computer music system); the lighting that would highlight the movements of the robots; the placement of the audience (around the robots); and the "theme," relating to the establishment of human rights (and, by extension, the rights of automatons). He envisaged an event of 20–30 minutes that could be repeated with programmed variations in the choreography based on stochastic functions.

In the end, Xenakis and Lohner worked for three years to find the funding and support for this tantalizing project. They approached automobile companies involved in automation research (Renault, Fiat), government agencies, attended industrial trade-shows, and so on. The first "occasion" that they tried to land funding for was the 1989 French bicentennial celebrations. This proved fruitless, as did all other opportunities in France, Germany, and Italy. By 1991, Xenakis dropped the project, no doubt with regret. But, in addition to numerous commissions (he completed an incredible 16 compositions in the period 1988–91, including six orchestral scores), he was involved in research at CEMAMu to develop software for stochastic digital synthesis and algorithmic composition (GENDYN).

Had they been able to return to the robotics project 10 years later, it would no doubt have been much more feasible, given the remarkable developments in the field of robotics and the subsequent lowering of technology costs. By 1997, however, Xenakis was no longer able to work due to ill health, and by 2001 he passed away.

Conclusion

In the years since his death, Xenakis's music has become even more attractive for choreographers. Dances have been set to his electroacoustic works, his music for solo percussion, and so on. One of the more ambitious projects is a choreographed version of *Oresteïa*. This work, a concert suite lasting approximately one hour, is scored for baritone soloist, percussion soloist, choir, children's choir, and instrumental ensemble. Choreographer Luca Veggetti combined six dancers with the live musicians for a 2008 production in New York, along with projections by photographer Pascal Delcey. *Oresteïa* is almost as long as *Kraanerg* (although clearly broken into seven sections), and utilizes more musicians.

Kraanerg has become established as a major work, to be performed as music, to be danced, to be combined with video and lighting. In a similar way, the music of Xenakis as a whole has become established as an important body of work representing an original creative vision arising from the struggles and possibilities

Epilogue

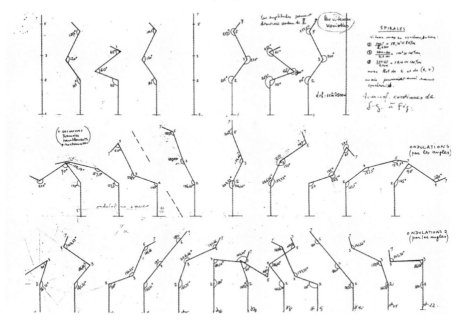

Figure 7.1   Sketches of robotic choreography by Xenakis (Xenakis Archives)

of the twentieth century. The "struggle for accomplishment and perfection" that *Kraanerg* seeks to embody can serve as a cornerstone for Xenakis's work in general. It also symbolizes a fundamental impulse of performers—musicians, dancers, etc.—to push themselves to surpass their abilities. Surely this helps to explain the growing attraction to his music by musicians and dancers both.

Bibliography

Barnes, Clive (1969), "Dance: Ballet by Xenakis opens Ottawa Arts Center," *New York Times* (4 June).
Beecroft, Norma (1981), "Xenakis à Toronto: Vision personnelle," in *Regards sur Iannis Xenakis*, Hugues Gerhards, editor (Paris: Stock, 1981), 315–19.
Bois, Mario (1966), *Iannis Xenakis, the Man and His Music: A Conversation with the Composer and a Description of His Work* (Paris: Boosey & Hawkes).
Boivin, Jean (1995), *La classe de Messaien* (Paris: Christian Bourgois).
Brown, Ismene (2011), "Roland Petit," *The Arts Desk* (10 July).
Le Corbusier (1954), *The Modulor* (Basel: Birkhäuser; first published in French, Boulogne-sur-Seine: Éditions de l'Architecture, 1950).
Connolley, Greg (1969), "National Arts Centre: A cultural equivalent to Bonaventure …?," *Ottawa Citizen* (30 May), 56.
Crisp, Clement (2011), "Roland Petit," *Financial Times* (27 July).
Cross, Jonathan (2005), *The Stravinsky Legacy* (Cambridge: Cambridge University Press).
DeLio, Thomas (1980), "The dialectics of structure and materials: Iannis Xenakis' *Nomos Alpha*," *Journal of Music Theory* 24 (1), 63–96.
Editorial (1969), "The National Arts Centre—Like 'Another Planet'," *Ottawa Journal* (3 June).
Fleuret, Maurice (1969), "Création de *Kraanerg* de Xenakis, R. Petit et Vasarely au Centre national des Arts d'Ottawa," *Nouvel Observateur* (17 June).
Foss, Lukas (1969), "Press release" (Ottawa: National Arts Centre, May).
Frisius, Rudolf (2003), "Musical et extramusical chez Xenakis. A propos de *Kraanerg* et de *Nekuïa*," in *Iannis Xenakis, Gérard Grisey: La métaphore lumineuse*, Makis Solomos, editor (Paris: L'Harmattan), 193–212.
Gibson, Benoît (2011), *The Instrumental Music of Iannis Xenakis: Theory, Practice, Self-Borrowing* (Hillsdale, NY: Pendragon).
Harley, James (2004), *Xenakis: His Life in Music* (New York: Routledge).
____ (2009), "Computational approaches to composition of notated instrumental music: Xenakis and other pioneers," in *The Oxford Handbook of Computer Music*, Roger Dean, editor (Oxford: Oxford University Press), 109–32.
____ (2011), "Nonlinear mosaic form: *Kraanerg* by Iannis Xenakis," in *Proceedings of the Xenakis International Symposium Southbank Centre, London, 1–3 April 2011* (www.gold.ac.uk/media/04.2 James Harley.pdf).
____ and Maria Anna Harley (1997), "Triumphs of modernity: Xenakis's *Kraanerg* at the National Arts Centre," *Musicworks* 76, 24–31.
Heller, Zelda (1969), "National Arts Centre: National Ballet of Canada," *Montreal Star* (3 June), 34–5.
Hicklin, Ralph (1969), "National Arts Centre debut: Ballet beats first-night novelty," *The Telegram* (3 June).

Hoad, Brian (1988), "Murphy's new journey," *The Bulletin* (22 November).
Kanach, Sharon (2008), *Music and Architecture by Iannis Xenakis* (Hillsdale, NY: Pendragon).
Kennedy, James (1972), "Canadian Ballet," *The Guardian* (22 May).
Lohner, Henning (1986), "Interview with Iannis Xenakis," *Computer Music Journal* 10 (4), 50–55.
Lombardo, Vincenzo, Andrea Valle, John Fitch, et al. (2009), "A virtual-reality reconstruction of *Poème électronique* based on philological research," *Computer Music Journal*, 33 (2), 24–47.
Mâche, François-Bernard (1993), "The Hellenism of Xenakis," *Contemporary Music Review*, 8 (1), 197–211.
Maeots, Krista (1969), "Completion was highlight," *Ottawa Citizen* (30 May), 58.
Matossian, Nouritza (1986), *Xenakis* (London: Kahn & Averill; first published in French, Paris: Fayard, 1981).
Miller, Malcolm (1993), "Xenakis's 'The Bacchae,'" *Tempo* 187 (December), 36–7.
Neufeld, James (2011), *Passion to Dance: The National Ballet of Canada* (Toronto: Dundurn).
Paparrigopoulos, Kostas (2006), "Western and Eastern approach of chance in the music of Xenakis and Cage: Theses and contra-theses," in *International Symposium Iannis Xenakis, Athens, May 2005, Definitive Proceedings*, Makis Solomos, Anastasia Georgaki, and Giorgos Zervos, editors (http://cicm.mshparisnord.org/ColloqueXenakis/papers/Paparrigopoulos.pdf).
Petit, Roland (1969a), "Press release" (Ottawa: National Arts Centre), May.
_____ (1969b), "Synopsis," *Kraanerg* program booklet (Ottawa: National Arts Centre/National Ballet of Canada).
Pritchett, James (1996), *The Music of John Cage* (Cambridge: Cambridge University Press).
Sargeant, Winthrop (1969), "Musical events," *The New Yorker* (15 February), 96–7.
Schaub, Stefan (2006), "*Akrata* for 16 winds by Iannis Xenakis: Analyses," in *International Symposium Iannis Xenakis, Athens, May 2005, Definitive Proceedings*, Makis Solomos, Anastasia Georgaki, and Giorgos Zervos, editors (http://cicm.mshparisnord.org/ColloqueXenakis/papers/Schaub.pdf).
Shoubridge, William (1988), "Dance: Murphy scores a thrilling success," *The Australian* (7 November).
Solomos, Makis (2009), "*Orient-Occident*: From the film version to the concert version," in *Iannis Xenakis: Das elektroakustische Werk*, Ralph Paland and Christoph von Blumröder, editors (Vienna: Apfel), 118–31.
Tennant, Veronica (2008), "Interview: On *Kraanerg*," Mode Records DVD 196.
Thistle, Lauretta (1969), "National Arts Centre Gala," *The Canadian Composer* (February).
Varga, Bálint András (1996), *Conversations with Iannis Xenakis* (London: Faber and Faber).

Vriend, Jan (1981), "'Nomos Alpha' for Violoncello Solo (Xenakis 1966): Analysis and Comments," *Interface* 10, 15–82.

Watson, Ben (1995), "Primal architect," *The Wire* 136 (June), 20–24.

Whittaker, Herbert (1969), "Petit's Kraanerg discloses dark vision of cosmic chaos," *Globe and Mail* (4 June).

Woodward, Roger (2010), "Conquering Goliath: Preparing and performing Xenakis' *Keqrops*," in *Performing Xenakis*, Sharon Kanach, editor (Hillsdale, NY: Pendragon), 129–55.

Xenakis, Françoise (1994), *Moi j'aime pas la mer* (Paris: Balland).

_____ (2008), "Interview: On *Kraanerg*," Mode Records DVD 196.

Xenakis, Iannis (1969), "Press release" (Ottawa: National Arts Centre, May).

_____ (1979), *Arts/Sciences, Alliages* (Tournai: Casterman; published in English as *Arts/Sciences, Alloys: The Thesis Defense of Iannis Xenakis*, translated by Sharon Kanach, Stuyvesant, NY: Pendragon, 1985).

_____ (1992), *Formalized Music*, revised edition (Hillsdale, NY: Pendragon; first published in English, Bloomington: Indiana University Press, 1971; first published in French as *Musiques formelles*, Paris: La Revue Musicale/Richard-Masse, 1963).

_____ (1994), "La crise de la musique sérielle," in *Kéleütha: Ecrits* (Paris: L'Arche), 39–43.

CD Track List

The recording of *Kraanerg* included here comes from the Mode Records 2008 release (Mode 196), featuring the Callithumpian Consort, conducted by Stephen Drury. The recording engineer was Toby Mountain, and the producers were Brian Brandt and Michael Hynes. The original recording has been edited by the author to create tracks that correspond to the start of each segment as discussed in Chapter 4. The timings on the disc do not exactly correspond to the timings noted in the score and discussed in the analysis (Chapter 4), but the tracks have been produced to mark the beginning of each segment as described in the book.

1. Ensemble Segment I — 0'34"
2. Playback Segment I — 2'11"
3. Ensemble Segment II — 0'39"
4. Playback Segment II — 2'21"
5. Ensemble Segment III — 1'41"
6. Playback Segment III — 0'38"
7. Ensemble Segment IV — 2'25"
8. Playback Segment IV — 0'55"
9. Ensemble Segment V — 2'52"
10. Playback Segment V — 1'29"
11. Ensemble Segment VI — 0'41"
12. Playback Segment VI — 1'43"
13. Ensemble Segment VII — 0'26"
14. Playback Segment VII — 1'19"
15. Ensemble Segment VIII — 2'23"
16. Playback Segment VIII — 1'14"
17. Ensemble Segment IX — 2'19"
18. Ensemble Segment X — 3'12"
19. Playback Segment IX — 0'55"
20. Playback Segment X — 0'33"
21. Ensemble Segment XI — 2'45"
22. Ensemble Segment XII — 1'09"
23. Ensemble Segment XIII — 2'00"
24. Playback Segment XI — 2'37"
25. Ensemble Segment XIV — 0'30"
26. Playback Segment XII — 2'12"

27. Ensemble Segment XV	1'36"
28. Playback Segment XIII	0'18"
29. Ensemble Segment XVI	0'41"
30. Playback Segment XIV	0'26"
31. Ensemble Segment XVII	1'01"
32. Ensemble Segment XVIII	2'39"
33. Playback Segment XV	0'23"
34. Ensemble Segment XIX	0'45"
35. Playback Segment XVI	0'33"
36. Ensemble Segment XX	3'23"
37. Playback Segment XVII	6'22"
38. Ensemble Segment XXI	0'21"
39. Playback Segment XVIII	0'32"
40. Ensemble Segment XXII	0'09"
41. Playback Segment XIX	0'35"
42. Ensemble Segment XXIII	7'02"
43. Ensemble Segment XXIV	2'13"
44. Playback Segment XX	6'14"

Index

abstraction 8, 13–14, 109
   sound spatialization 9, 14–15, 33–4, 44, 45, 72, 75, 86, 98, 100, 104
Achorripsis (1957) 11–12, 16–17, 20–21, 22
À Colone (1977) 30
Aeschylus 13, 29
Agostini, P. 11
À Hélène (1977) 30
Aïs (1980) 5, 91
Akrata (1965) 27, 53, 54, 60, 63
Alpha Centauri Ensemble 115, 117
Amorsima-Morsima (1962) 23
Anaktoria (1969) 1
Analogique A & B (1958–1959) 12, 16, 24
Anastenaria 8
Antikhthon (1971) 30–31, 114, 123
architecture 1, 4, 14, 24, 31–4, 104, 120 *see also* Le Corbusier
   installations *see* installations
   Philips Pavilion 1, 6, 11, 31, 33–4
Asko/Schönberg Ensemble 120
Atrées (1962/3) 16, 23, 31
   Private Domain 31
attack points 10, 20
Avignon Festival 1

Balanchine, G. 30–31, 40, 113, 114, 123
Barraqué, J. 7
Barrault, J.-L. 13
Bartók, B. 8
Béjart, M. 1, 31, 109
Berio, L. 1, 16
Bohor (1962) 12–13, 30, 34, 44, 75, 104
Boosey & Hawkes 35, 42, 43, 103, 104, 111
Bornstein, C.Z. 114, 118
Boucourechliev, A. 7
Boulanger, N. 7
Boulez, P. 9, 16
Brussels World Fair (1958) 1, 11, 31

Cage, J. 21, 117
Callithumpian Consort 114, 117, 120, 131
Carter, E. 16

CEMAMu (Centre d'Études de Mathématique et Automatique Musicales) 23, 45, 124
Chalon, G. 45
chance procedures 21
Charisma (1971) 96
compositional process 19–20, 46, 53
   computer algorithms 21–3
   formalization 19–21
   final symbolic result 19
   fundamental phases, computer algorithm, as 21
   groups 21–6 *see also* group theory
   implementation of calculations 19
   initial conceptions 19, 20, 22
   Kraanerg, of *see Kraanerg*
   microcomposition 19, 20
   sequential programming 19
   sieves 24–6 *see also* sieves
   sonic entities 19 *see also* sonic entities
   sonic realization 19
   stochastic procedures in 2, 10, 12, 15, 20, 24, 29 *see also* stochastic procedures
   transformations, definition of 19 *see also* transformations
compositional techniques 10, 27, 89
computer algorithms 21–3, 28, 89, 124 *see also* compositional process
   fundamental compositional phases as 21
computer music 2, 22, 23, 29, 124 *see also* digital sound synthesis; electroacoustic music
Concret PH 11, 34, 75, 104, 113
Constant, M. 38–9, 40, 41, 45, 103, 113, 114, 117
Copland, A. 16, 29
Cunningham, M. 50, 107, 112
Cycle Xenakis 114

dance music 30–31
Decoust, M. 7
Deutsches Nationaltheater Weimar 118
Diamorphoses (1957) 11, 104

Dieudonné, A. 7
digital sound synthesis 23, 29, 124 *see also* computer music; electroacoustic music
   filtering 72
   gain adjustment 72
   pitch alteration 72
   reverberation 72
documentary film scores 12
Donaueschingen Festival 1, 9
Drury, S. 114, 117, 120, 131
Duel 12, 14

East West Music Encounter Conference 1961 16
electroacoustic music 1, 12, 16, 29, 30, 34, 44, 45, 63, 75, 103, 104, 119
   choreographing 124
   first 11
electronic music 9, 11, 15, 44
EMAMu (Équipe de Mathématique et d'Automatique Musicales) 1, 22, 23
   CEMAMu (Centre d'Études de Mathématique et Automatique Musicales) 23, 45, 124
   establishment 23
   opening 1, 23
Ensemble Ars Nova 41, 45, 103, 104, 113, 114, 117
Eonta (1964) 14, 16, 17, 24, 34, 54
   Them and Us 31
Euripides 13, 123
Expo 67 1, 15, 32, 34, 37

Fibonacci series 8
first monograph concert 16–17
Formalized Music 10, 19, 24, 26, 29
Foss, L. 29, 35
   Kraanerg, conducting 42, 46, 103 *see also Kraanerg*
Freeman, D. 13, 123
Fulchignoni, E. 12

game theory 12, 14
Garant, S. 7
Genuys, F. 22, 23

Grand Prix de l'Académie du Disque Français 17
group theory 24, 26, 29, 53, 54, 89, 94
   constraints 27
   inside time 24, 26 *see also* inside time
Groupe de Recherches Musicales (GRM) 8–9, 11, 12, 13, 44–5, 103, 113

Henry, P. 1, 9
Herma (1961) 16, 24
Hibiki-Hana-Ma (1970) 16, 75, 86
Hiller, L. 22
   Illiac Suite (1957) 22–3
Honegger, A. 7

IBM-France 22
   computer access 23
   concert at 23
inside time 24, 26–9
installations 15, 32
   Le Diatope 33 *see also Le Diatope*
   Polytope de Montréal (1967) 32–4, 41, 44 *see also Polytope de Montréal* (1967)
intervallic relationships 24, 25, 26, 90
Isaacson, L. 22

Jolas, B. 7
Jonchaies (1977) 17, 114
Journées de Musique Contemporaine (Paris, 1968) 1

Kammerensemble Neue Musik Berlin 119
Keqrops (1986) 115
Kluttig, R. 119
Korolkoff, Y. 45
Kötter, D. 119
Kraanerg (1969) 13, 19, 20, 29, 30, 31, 34, 35, 53, 124
   attack points 100, 101
   ballet performances 43, 103, 111, 112 *see also premiere below*
   Canada, in 119
   choreographers 42, 46, 103, 115, 118, 119
   critics 108–10, 112, 113, 115–16, 118

designers 42, 46, 103, 118
Europe, in 117–18, 119
Sydney, in 115–17
commissioning 41, 53
compositional process 53–4, 60
concert performances 113–14, 118, 120
electroacoustic component 44–5,
   54–5, 60, 62, 63, 72, 103 *see also*
   electroacoustic music
  amplitude, playback material, of
    75–86
  layers of 86
  recording 45, 72
formal design 60–63, 86–9
Grand Prix du Disque 113
hybrid performances 119–20
instrumentation 42–3
Part One 89–92
  ES (ensemble segment) I 89, 90
  ES II 89, 92
  ES III 89–90
  ES IV 90, 92
  ES V 90, 91
  ES VI 91
  ES VII 91
  ES VIII 91, 93, 94
  PS (playback segment) I 89
  PS II 89
  PS III 90
  PS IV 90, 91
  PS V 91
  PS VI 91
  PS VII 91
  PS VIII 92
Part Three 98–101
  ES XXI 99
  ES XXII 99
  ES XXIII 99
  ES XXIV 99–100
  PS XVIII 99
  PS XIX 99, 100
  PS XX 100
Part Two 92–8
  ES IX 92, 93
  ES X 92–3, 94
  ES XI 93–4
  ES XII 94, 95, 98

  ES XIII 93, 94, 95, 98
  ES XIV 93, 95
  ES XV 93, 95–6
  ES XVI 96
  ES XVII 96, 97
  ES XVIII 96, 97
  ES XIX 97
  ES XX 97–8, 100
  PS IX 92, 93
  PS X 93, 96
  PS XI 93, 95
  PS XII 93, 95, 98
  PS XIII 93, 96
  PS XIV 96–7
  PS XV 97
  PS XVI 97
  PS XVII 98
premiere 1, 103, 105, 106, 107–8, 123
  see also ballet performances above
  choreographer 42, 46, 103
  choreography 46, 48–51, 62–3, 95,
    116
  conductor 42, 46, 103
  critics 108–10, 112, 113
  designer 42, 46, 103
recordings 104, 113, 117, 118–19, 120
restoration of original 119
spatialization of 75–86
score 44, 54–60, 74, 103, 106,
  Annexes 101–2
segments 60, 62, 63, 64–7, 86 *see also*
  Parts above
  blocks 62, 63, 88, 92, 93, 94–5, 97,
    99
  ensemble 60–62, 63, 64, 72, 87–8,
    99–100
  markers 94
  playback 62, 64, 72, 75–86, 87–8,
    93, 99–100
silence in 92, 94, 95, 96, 98
sketches for 53–4, 60, 63, 72, 75
sonic entities 68–71
sonic mosaic, as 60, 63, 88–9, 100–101
soloists 42, 48
stage design 46–8
Koundourov, A. 4
Kyoto Prize 16

Laporte, G. 45
Laroux, B. 45
Lebensold, F. 35–6, 104
Le Corbusier 1, 6, 8, 11, 12, 31, 36
    Poème électronique 11, 15, 34
    Le Diatope: La Légende d'Eer (1978) 15, 33, 34, 86
    Le Sacrifice (1953) 8, 9
Leimbach, F. 118
Les Percussions de Strasbourg 1
Ligeti, G. 10
Lohner, H. 123, 124
London Opera Factory 13

Maceda, J. 16, 21
Mâche, F.-B. 7
Maderna, B. 12
Magnanensi, G. 114, 119
Markov chains 24
Mathews, M. 23, 29
Medea 13, 41, 90, 104
Méfano, P. 114
Mehta, Z. 115
Menny, B. 45
Messiaen, O. 7, 8, 9, 19, 38
metabolae 25
Metastaseis (1954) 8, 10, 11, 13, 17, 19, 30, 40, 101
    premiere 1, 9
Milhaud, D. 7, 38
Mists (1980) 115
modulus 24–5
Morsima-Amorsima (1962) 23
multi-channel sound 12, 15, 16, 30, 33, 34, 44, 72, 75, 86, 100, 119
    playback 76–85, 89, 103, 120
multimedia works 1–2, 6, 11, 14, 15, 23, 34, 44, 119, 123 *see also* polytopes
Murphy, G. 115–16, 117, 118
Musica Viva Festival (Munich 1957) 10

National Arts Centre, Ottawa (NAC) 35–8, 104
    controversial architecture 104
    inauguration 104–5
    opening gala 38, 40, 42, 103, 105, 106–8 *see also Kraanerg*
    sound system 44
National Ballet of Canada 35, 37–8, 106
    Kraanerg 43, 109–10, 111, 112 *see also Kraanerg*
    performance rights 111
New York City Ballet 30
New York Philharmonic 115
Nomos alpha (1966) 1, 26, 27–8, 31, 53, 54, 89, 101
Nomos gamma (1968) 1, 15, 29, 31, 34, 44, 53, 54, 63, 72, 73, 74, 104
Nuits 54, 72
Nyuyo (1985) 16

Octuor de Paris 1
Orchestre Philharmonique de Luxembourg 120
Oresteïa 13. 29–30, 41, 104, 113, 123, 124
Orient-Occident 12
Osaka World Fair (1970) 16
outside time 24, 26–9
Ozawa, S. 16, 42

parameters 19, 24, 53, 54, 60
    qualities 62
    shifts 60, 62, 63, 88–9
    value sets 26
parametrical elements 26
    parametrical synchronicity 63
Penderecki, K. 10
Persephassa (1969) 1, 15
Persepolis (1971) 15, 86
Petit, J. 11
Petit, R. 35, 38–41, 46, 106–7, 118
    Kraanerg, choreographing 42, 48–9, 50, 63, 95 *see also Kraanerg*
Philips Corporation 11
pitch 10, 19–20, 22, 91, 92, 94, 96, 101
    alteration 45, 72, 75, 93
    collections 24
    fixed 60, 63, 89, 90, 93
    modes 24
    neighbor 90, 92, 93

range 62, 63, 96
secondary element, as 22
sieves 26 *see also* sieve theory
Pithoprakta (1956) 10, 11, 16, 17, 19, 21, 30, 40
Polla ta Dhina (1962) 13
polytopes 1, 15, 119, 123 *see also* multimedia works
  architecture and 31–4
Polytope de Cluny (1972) 1–2, 15, 29, 86
Polytope de Montréal (1967) 1, 15, 32–4, 41, 44, 53, 75, 104
Polytope de Mycènes (1978) 15
Pour la Paix (1982) 44
Procession vers les eaux claires (1953) 8
Psappha (1975) 5

quilisma 53, 91, 94, 96, 97, 100, 101

Radio France (ORTF) 9, 35, 41, 45, 103
recordings, *Kraanerg*, of 104, 113, 117, 118–19,
  DVD 120
Reservoir 118
rhythm 2, 10, 13, 24, 100
  cross- 91, 93, 99
  layered 95
  secondary element, as 22
  sieves 24 *see also* sieve theory
Riopelle, J.-P. 40
robotics 123–4, 125
Rosbaud, H. 9
Royan Festival 1, 9, 31, 34

Salle Gaveau 1965 16–17
Samuel, C. 114
Schaeffer, P. 8–9, 13
Scherchen, H. 8, 9–10, 12, 19, 21
Schlömer, J. 118
serialism 8, 9–10, 21
Shiraz Festival (Iran) 1, 15
sieve theory 24–5, 26 *see also* transformations
  outside time 24 *see also* outside time
  pitch sieve 24, 26

Simonovitch, C. 12, 16, 21
Sinfonieorchester Basel 118
sketches 27, 123, 124
  Kraanerg 53–4, 60, 63, 72, 75 see also *Kraanerg*
Solomos, A. 13, 29
sonic entities 19, 21, 22, 24, 26, 53, 62, 68–71, 88–9
  transformations of 20 *see also* transformations
sonority 2, 8, 21, 43 49–50, 53, 63, 72, 88, 91–2, 93–4, 96, 101
sound spatialization 14–15, 33–4, 44, 45, 72, 75, 86, 98, 100, 104
ST pieces 24, 29
  ST/4 (1962) 23, 101
  ST/10 (1962) 16, 23
  ST/48 (1962) 23
ST-X Ensemble 114, 117, 118
stochastics 2, 10, 12, 15, 20, 22, 24, 29, 124
  see also compositional process
  clouds 19
  Markov chains 24
Stockhausen, K. 7, 12
  Klavierstücke XI 12
Strasbourg, Les Percussions de 1
Stratégie (1962) 12, 14, 16
Stravinsky, I. 16, 30
Strobel, H. 9
Studio Acousti 35, 45, 103
SudWestFunk Radio Orchestra 9
Sydney Dance Company 115 *see also* *Kraanerg*, ballet performances
Syrmos (1959) 12, 16, 41, 104

Tabachnik, M. 17
Takahashi, Y. 16
Takemitsu, T. 16
Tamayo, A. 114, 120
Tanglewood Music Center 29, 31
  Summer Music Festival 1963 16
Taylor, P. 31
Teige, D. 119
Terretektorh (1966) 9, 15, 34, 104

texture 2, 9, 10, 13, 15, 21, 54, 60, 63, 72,
    92, 95, 97, 100, 102
  composite 75, 94
  density 90, 91
  mixed 92, 93, 94, 95, 97, 99, 100
  shifts 88, 97–8
  sustained 88, 89, 90, 91, 93, 94, 96, 97,
    98, 99–100
The Bacchae 13, 123
The Suppliants 13, 15
theory of music 19
transformations 19, 20, 26, 72–5
  constrained 26
  interval sets, of 26
  metabolae 25
Tremblay, M. 105
Tuorakemsu (1990) 16

Varèse, E. 1, 11, 19–20
  Déserts 8, 9
  Poème électronique 11, 15, 34
Vasarely, V. 35, 42, 46, 103
  Kraanerg, designing 42, 47 *see also*
    Kraanerg
Venice Biennale (1962) 12
Vilella, E. 40, 42

Wakasugi, H. 16
Waltz, S. 119
Woodward, R. 115, 117
World Exposition, Montréal (1967) 1, 15,
    32, 34, 37
Wyss, P. 117–18
  Lulu-Szenen 117
  Oedipus, der Mensch 117–18

Xenakis, F. 8, 123
Xenakis, I. 3, 14
  Athens Polytechnic 4–5
  birth 3
  breakthrough 9–11
  Communist Party, and 5, 6
  controversy over 17
  dance, and 30–31
  death 124
  doctoral thesis 26
  documentary film scores 12
  early compositions 7–8
  early years 3–4
  exile 5, 6–7, 13
  first monograph concert 16
  Grand Prix de l'Académie du Disque
    Français 17
  Greek Resistance, and 5
  influence of 2, 119
  influences on 7–8, 12, 19–20
  Kraanerg see Kraanerg
  Kyoto Prize 16
  Le Corbusier, and 6, 11 *see also* Le
    Corbusier
  publications 9–10, 19, 26, 31
    Formalized Music 10, 19, 24, 26, 29
  reputation 16–17
  research 29
  teaching 16, 29
  technical abilities 13
  WWII, during 5
Xenakis, M. 8